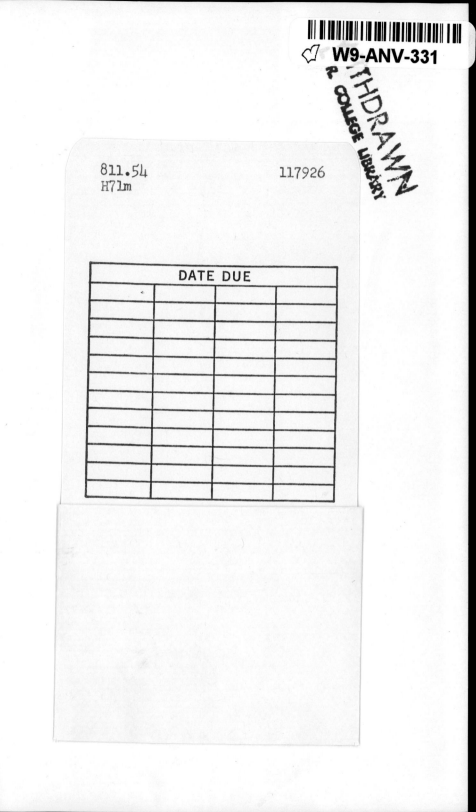

The Mark to Turn

William Stafford

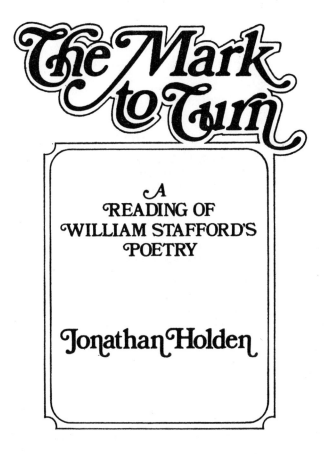

The Mark to Turn

A
**READING OF
WILLIAM STAFFORD'S
POETRY**

Jonathan Holden

THE UNIVERSITY PRESS OF KANSAS
Lawrence/Manhattan/Wichita

© Copyright 1976 by the University Press of Kansas
Printed in the United States of America
Designed by Fritz Reiber

Library of Congress Cataloging in Publication Data
Holden, Jonathan.
The mark to turn.

Bibliography: p.
Includes index.
1. Stafford, William Edgar, 1914-
—Criticism and interpretation. I. Title.
PS3537.T143Z7   811'.5'4   76-2024
ISBN 0-7006-0145-7
ISBN 0-7006-0146-5 pbk.

Quotations from the following books are used by
permission of Harper & Row, Publishers, Inc.:
TRAVELING THROUGH THE DARK by William
Stafford, Copyright © 1962 by William Stafford;
THE RESCUED YEAR by William Stafford, Copy-
right © 1966 by William E. Stafford; ALLE-
GIANCES by William Stafford, Copyright © 1970
by William E. Stafford; SOMEDAY, MAYBE by
William Stafford, Copyright © 1973 by William
Stafford.

Acknowledgments

The author is grateful to Harper & Row for permission to use quotations from Stafford's books *Traveling through the Dark, The Rescued Year, Allegiances,* and *Someday, Maybe*; and to William Stafford for permission to quote from *West of Your City.* I also wish to express deep gratitude to James Pirie, of the Lewis and Clark College Library, for his generosity in letting me use the tremendous collection of writings by or about Stafford which he has compiled, and for letting me use the index to it. This index comprises the best extant Stafford bibliography. I also wish to express gratitude to my various friends and colleagues whose interest in this book and whose hard-nosed suggestions have helped me to shape and refine it. I am particularly indebted to James Folsom, John Wrenn, Lee Krauth, Tom Dillingham, and Reg Saner.

Contents

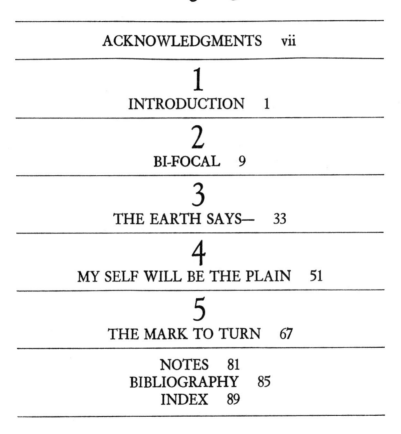

I do tricks in order to know:
careless I dance,
then turn to see
the mark to turn God left for me.

—WILLIAM STAFFORD

Abbreviations

Throughout this book, the following abbreviations will be employed for Stafford's poetry collections:

WOYC	*West of Your City*
TTD	*Traveling through the Dark*
RY	*The Rescued Year*
A	*Allegiances*
SM	*Someday, Maybe*

Introduction

In 1970, in *Field*, William Stafford wrote:

> At times, without my insisting on it, my writings become coherent; the successive elements that occur to me are clearly related. They lead by themselves to new connections. Sometimes the language, even the syllables that happen along, may start a trend. Sometimes the materials alert me to something waiting in my mind, ready for sustained attention. At such times I allow myself to be eloquent, or intentional, or for great swoops (treacherous! not to be trusted!) reasonable. But I do not insist on any of that; for I know that back of my activity there will be the coherence of my self, and that indulgence of my impulses will bring recurrent patterns and meanings again.[1]

My aim in this reading of Stafford's poems is to demonstrate the coherence of his work as a whole, to isolate what I believe to be the major "patterns" and "meanings" which recur throughout it.

Stafford's opus is so large that, for the sake of economy, I have restricted the scope of this book to his first published collection of poems, *West of Your City*, and to his four major poetry collections published by Harper & Row. These books comprise a relatively small fraction of his published work, but

they are relatively accessible, and, from them alone, the interlocking set of metaphors which constructs Stafford's vision may
be readily generalized.[2]

One must keep in mind, when considering Stafford's books,
that, although each book is thematically organized, the chronological order in which they have appeared bears only a casual
relationship to the order in which the poems were written. For
example, *The Rescued Year* (1966), Stafford's third collection
and his second published by Harper & Row, includes fourteen
of the poems from *West of Your City* (1960).[3] Thus *The
Rescued Year* contains some poems written at least six years
earlier. Some of them are even older. "Bi-focal," for example,
was included in *Winterward*, the creative Ph.D. thesis Stafford
completed under Ray West at the University of Iowa, in 1954.
"Ozymandias's Brother," which appears in Stafford's latest collection, *Someday, Maybe* (1973), is one of the poems which
the poet Donald Hall, who has had a limited hand in editing
the manuscripts for Stafford's Harper & Row collections, cut
from the manuscript of *The Rescued Year*. Since Stafford's
books, then, do not accurately represent the chronological,
thematic, or stylistic development of the poems included, I have
selected for discussion those poems most convenient for explica-
tion, in an order wholly independent of the books in which
they originally appeared.

A second reason why I have ignored chronology is to pre-
serve the integrity of Stafford's vision. Although many of his
poems are based upon personal memories, as these memories
are situated throughout the books, they form a rather haphazard
mosaic, not a linear story. Stafford himself is aware of this.
In an interview in *Courier*, he says: "For me, the past and the
present and in fact to make a claim, the future, all seem to be
simultaneous. That is, writing is a sort of venturing forward
easily in a welcoming way in terms of your immediate experience, but that immediate experience carries with it many echoes
from the past."[4] This non-linear relationship between the
present and the past is such an integral part of Stafford's vision

that to attempt to disassemble the mosaic and chronologically reorder the pieces would be to crucially misrepresent Stafford's intentions.

A third reason why I have ignored the chronology of his poems is to de-emphasize their apparent biographical significance. For example, sprinkled throughout the books are some poems which allude nostalgically to an "Ella." When I asked Stafford who Ella might be, he insisted that, although he had known in his youth a girl named Ella, the Ella of his poems was a fictional composite of many girls that he remembered. Stafford's poem "Homecoming" (*RY*, 13), one of the poems originally included in *Winterward*, bears him out. The version in *The Rescued Year* begins:

> Under my hat I custom you intricate, Ella;
> at homecoming I glance and remember your street.
> "What happened to Ella?" they ask, asking too fast;
> so I fold them off, thousands of answers deep.

In the *Winterward* version, however, Ella is named "Goldie." Stafford's explanation to me of this is that when he was attending the Iowa Writers Workshop, there was a general consensus among the participants that poems should contain strong elements of realism. He was persuaded that "Ella" was too ethereal a name. "Ella," then, stands for something evanescent, perhaps, as the title "Homecoming" suggests, the spirit of a place in the past, of the small, Kansas towns where Stafford grew up.

As "Homecoming" indicates, it is dangerous to treat a Stafford poem as literal biography. An example of the type of error that a biographical interpretation can produce may be seen in Karen Sollid's discussion of "Some Shadows" (*RY*, 4).[5]

"Some Shadows" immediately impresses one as more melodramatic than most of Stafford's notably quiet poetry. The speaker of the poem is tense, grimly self-pitying. He is apologizing to the reader for being "reserved" and "cold." He explains that he is this way because his life was hard as a child:

"When Mother was a girl Indians/ shadowed that country, the barren lands./ Mother ran to school winter mornings/ with hot potatoes in her hands." The tone becomes increasingly bitter as he describes his parents' marriage and his father:

> A lean man, a cruel, took her [Mother].
> I am his son.
>
> He was called Hawk by the town people,
> but was an ordinary man.
> He lived by trapping and hunting
> wherever the old slough ran.
>
> .   .   .   .
>
> Forgive me these shadows I cling to, good people,
> trying to hold quiet in my prologue.
> Hawks cling the barrens wherever I live.
> The world says, "Dog eat dog."

Sollid gives the poem a biographical interpretation:

> In "Some Shadows," . . . he [Stafford] opens his book and the poem with Stafford-direct statements about his conception of his past world: . . . And later, in the closing lines of the same poem, he tries to indicate the enormous difference between how he remembers the world of his childhood and the world that he knows and understands as a man now: . . . He recognizes that there is reason for the difficulty he has adjusting to the world of "Dog eat dog."[6]

She misreads the poem because she assumes that the speaker is Stafford himself, remembering his own childhood. But Stafford's father did not live by "trapping"; and given Stafford's propriety—the strictness with which he avoids sordid, personal confession in his poems—it would be astonishing were he to refer to his own father as a "cruel" man.

In fact, Stafford told me, the speaker of "Some Shadows" is a *persona*. As the poem's title, "Some Shadows," might suggest, the speaker is a shade, a ghost. Like Ella, this shadow is the spirit of a place in the past, but a past far more remote than the past which Ella inhabits, a past now mythical to Stafford, when Kansas was barely settled and "Indians/ shadowed that country." Stafford is consciously inventing and savoring a legend he would like to have had a share in, a legend about the region where he was raised. The poem is *not* about Stafford's recognizing "that there is reason for the difficulty he has adjusting to the world."

Another and final example of the limitations in a biographical approach to Stafford's poetry is his poem "Montana Eclogue" (*A*, 28–30). The speaker of the poem is Stafford himself. The setting is autumn. Stafford, who has "stopped indoors," imagines that winter is already flooding into the mountains of Montana. The second stanza begins:

> Logue, the man who always closes down the camp,
> is left all alone at Clear Lake, where
> he is leisurely but busy, pausing to glance across
> the water toward Winter Peak. The bunkhouse
> will be boarded up, the cookshack barricaded
> against bears, the corral gates lashed shut.

These lines convey the impression that Stafford is describing a place he has visited; perhaps he spent a summer vacation at this camp, and Logue is a man he has known personally. According to Stafford, however, Logue is an entirely fictional invention. The name, which echoes the "Eclogue" of the poem's title, Stafford chose because he liked the sound of it. The actual occasion of the poem was Stafford's reading in a newspaper that some "camps" in Montana were closing down for the winter. Like Ella and the hardbitten *persona* of "Some Shadows," Logue is the spirit of a place, a legendary figure invented by Stafford as a metaphorical link to a domain reared in the imagination. Stafford puts this clearly in the next stanza: "And Logue, by being there, suddenly/ carries for us everything that we can load on him."

It would be foolish to deny that many of Stafford's poems such as "The Rescued Year" contain biographical material; but it should not be given the weight or attention it would deserve were Stafford, like Robert Lowell, an avowedly confessional poet. Generally, in a Stafford poem biographical content is placed wholly in the service of imagination, as material for fiction.

The imagination—its resilience, its stubborn and playful instinct for deriving meaning and awe from the world—is the central theme of Stafford's work. In this respect, despite profound differences in style, Stafford's poetry bears perhaps a closer affinity to the poetry of Wallace Stevens than to that of any other recent American poet. It exhibits a steady consciousness of Romantic tradition, particularly Wordsworth and Thoreau. Like Stevens's, Stafford's Romanticism is stylized, abstract, and always informed by a controlling intelligence. Stafford is not considered, as Stevens is, a "difficult" poet; his poems exhibit none of the studied, elegant artificiality of a Stevens poem. Most of them move with the apparent artlessness of a great centerfielder drifting back to make the catch of a slicing line-drive look routine. Stafford rarely seems to work hard in a poem, to contrive his results, to wring, as James Dickey often does, more adventitious significance out of a poem than its occasion warrants. In his interviews as well as in his poems, Stafford likes to promote a picture of himself as naïve.

In fact, however, his poems and his conception of poetry are extremely sophisticated. A deft, alert intellect exhibits itself everywhere in his work—through his frequent etymological use of words, through puns, through the construction of deliberate but carefully limited ambiguities and through a scrupulous New-Critical attention to consistency.

Despite his sophistication, Stafford's stance as a writer is democratic, informed by a strong sense of commonality with other human beings. This sense accounts for much of his stylization. Most of his poems are spoken by a "we" rather than an "I." Some are even addressed to "you." Many of them are

openly didactic. "Watching the Jet Planes Dive" (*WOYC*, 37),
for example, is spoken from a sermonic stance:

> We must go back and find a trail on the ground
> back of the forest and mountain on the slow land;
> we must begin to circle on the intricate sod.

As this passage indicates, the physical world, where it is represented in a Stafford poem, is conspicuously bare and abstract.
The generalized quality of Stafford's imagery, although it occasionally leaves the reader thirsting for more concrete richness
of detail, yields one considerable benefit: the reader is rarely
kept, through unfamiliarity with some topical detail, from
sharing the experience of a poem. The poems may thus convincingly address a community. Paradoxically, however, the
stark, abstract terms from which Stafford constructs his poems,
while their surface simplicity invites the reader into an apparently artless world, comprise a highly specialized vocabulary in
which certain words recur with a cryptic and figurative significance. This figurative significance, though not immediately
obvious, is rigorously consistent throughout his work. Such
words as "deep," "dark," "cold," "God," "home," "near," and
"far" Stafford consciously uses as a symbolic shorthand, as components in that set of interlocking metaphors which defines his
vision of the world.

Stafford's vision, although it comprehends paradox, is not
particularly complicated. And it is precise—far more precise
than Stafford's comments or prevalent critical opinion would
have us believe. When critics praise Stafford's poetry, it is
often because they seem to find it agreeably vague. For example, M. L. Rosenthal, in *The New Poets*, refers to "the
elusively impressionistic William Stafford";[7] and in an interview with Stafford, Lewis Turco remarks: "I think Mr. Stafford's work is resonant. Rather than having it finished and
closed ended, and rather than having it simply hang, it resonates; the poem's meaning amplifies."[8] Few would quarrel
with Turco's praise of "resonance" in poetry; but after repeated

close reading of Stafford's poems, "resonance" is the last quality I would single out to *emphasize*. In fact, by contemporary standards, Stafford's poems are relatively *closed*-ended and contain a relatively high proportion of didactic content. Stafford's didactic quality, however, does not immediately stand out, because his poems are frequently so cryptic. Without some grasp of Stafford's specialized vocabulary, it is impossible to make much of the ending of a poem like "So Long" (*A*, 82):

> No one can surface till far,
> far on, and all that we'll have
> to love may be what's near
> in the cold, even then.

Why are Stafford's poems often this oblique? Perhaps it is to soften their didactic element which runs directly against current taste. It is virtually dogma today that the more easily the reader can abstract a poem's content the worse the poem is, that explicitly didactic verse barely deserves the name "poetry." Being cryptic is one way to insure that you are not obvious. It is one of the possible methods by which a poet can practice what W. D. Snodgrass has labeled "tact."[9]

Sometimes, as in the end of "So Long," Stafford's shorthand is too abbreviated. If the reader is not familiar with Stafford's use of "surface," "far," "near," and "cold" in many other contexts, the poem will do nothing for him *except* "resonate." By examining elements of Stafford's symbolic vocabulary, I would like to demonstrate that his poems do more than that: they exhibit, in a tremendously compressed form, a coherent moral vision of the world.

Bi-focal

A poem which introduces many of the basic elements of Stafford's vision and his vocabulary is "Bi-focal" (*WOYC*, 44; *RY*, 63). As its title implies, the theme of "Bi-focal" is double vision—the double vision upon which virtually all of Stafford's poems are grounded. The poem reads:

> Sometimes up out of this land
> a legend begins to move.
> Is it a coming near
> of something under love?
>
> Love is of the earth only,
> the surface, a map of roads
> leading wherever go miles
> or little bushes nod.
>
> Not so the legend under,
> fixed, inexorable,
> deep as the darkest mine
> the thick rocks won't tell.
>
> As fire burns the leaf
> and out of the green appears
> the vein in the center line
> and the legend veins under there,

So, the world happens twice—
once what we see it as;
second it legends itself
deep, the way it is.

Like many of Stafford's poems, "Bi-focal" is built around one word which in the context of the poem assumes an increasingly complex significance. Here, the word is "legend." In the first stanza, it is used in its modern sense, as an unverifiable but generally known story. "Move" suggests "spread," which implies that the "legend" begins to assume credibility and currency.

The source of the "legend" is "this land." The story comes "up out of" it, from "under" the "surface." In the third stanza, "legend" assumes additional connotations: it is "fixed, inexorable,/ deep as the darkest mine." "Fixed" implies both that it is prescribed and that it is already set down. The Latin origin of "legend" suggests also that the legend is inscribed. "Inexorable" gives it a dynamic aspect. The legend is relentless. The Latin sense of "inexorable" implies that it is cryptic. We pray to it, entreat it to yield up its meaning; but it will not answer, will not be translated.

The image of the legend as written is reinforced by the leaf image in the fourth stanza. When a leaf burns, its veins reveal themselves as a calligraph. The use of "veins" as a verb prefigures the poem's final strategy. The legend is a dynamic process which "veins" itself in a burning leaf.

In the final stanza, Stafford gives "legend" its last twist by using it as a verb. The natural world, through rocks, through the leaf, is emblematic of a prescribed story—an unfolding process—which is writing itself, a story which is inexorable because it can be neither stopped nor interpreted. We cannot interpret it because we do not know its ending and because it "legends itself/ deep": that part of the story which has already been set down is inscribed "under" the "surface" of things, inside "thick rocks." Stafford's ultimate use of "legends" as a verb implies not only that the "world" is writing its story, but that it is reading what it sets down. This implication, reinforced by the personifications "bushes nod" and "the thick rocks won't tell," attributes to the natural world a faintly Wordsworthian suggestion of consciousness.

Although Stafford never uses, as Wordsworth does, the word "Nature" in a poem, a distinction between man and Nature is always implicit, as in the last stanza of "Bi-focal," where the first-person pronoun "we" is introduced. In the clause "once what we see it [the world] as," "we" is the subject and "it" is the direct object of "see." The syntax of that clause thus posits a subject-object relation between "us" and the natural world of "rock," "leaf," and "land."

The word "near" in the first stanza deserves particular attention. The distinction which Stafford makes between man and Nature is one which, throughout his work, he systematically represents in terms of physical distance. This distance metaphor is basic to his vision. In general, the degree of *felt difference of identity* which Stafford wishes to express between himself and Nature is represented, in a given poem, as physical distance. This "distance" may vary. The greater the distance, the greater his feeling of difference—of Nature's otherness. The less this distance, the greater his feeling of kinship. "Bi-focal" is one of the comparatively few Stafford poems in which Nature is represented as "near," in which Stafford expresses a pronounced feeling of kinship with the earth. The personifications such as "the thick rocks won't tell" which abound in Stafford's poems do not serve to promote a vision of the similarities between Nature and man; they serve as a constant and implicit reminder of the differences. "The thick rocks won't tell," although it attributes a glimmer of consciousness to Nature, represents that consciousness as radically other than human consciousness. It is inexorable.

Two other metaphors central to Stafford's vision are introduced in "Bi-focal"—the words "deep" and "dark." In context, "deep" is opposed to "surface." It is also defined. "Deep" is "the way it [the world] is." If "deep" is the way the world *is*, then its "surface" is not. "Deep" is also associated with "dark." As the connotations of "deep" suggest, that which is "deep" is "dark" because it cannot be visualized; it is written inside the natural world, "under" the surface where the eye cannot penetrate.

If the domain of the "deep" is "dark," then, by inference, "surface" is associated with light, with what *is* visible to the eye, with finite spatial relations, with "map[s]," "roads," "miles." "Deep," then, in its opposition to "surface," is implicitly associated with time rather than space. "The thick rocks won't tell" implies that the time-span of the world's legend has a geological scale, a scale of such immensity that it cannot be visualized. As the very word "legend"—an *unverifiable* story, one which must be accepted on faith—implies, it is "dark" because it can only be imagined.

"Dark," then, and images of darkness such as "night" are Stafford's primary metaphors for the invisible, for what can be apprehended only through the imagination. They correspond to that obscurity which, throughout Romantic poetry and particularly in the poems of Wordsworth and Coleridge, liberates the imagination and allows it free play.

Stafford's conscious deployment of "dark" to symbolize "invisible" is evident in a poem such as his "Like a Little Stone" (*A*, 50), which, in the last stanza, equates "darkness" with "all possibilities":

> If time won't let a thing happen, hurry there,
> to the little end of the cone that darkness bends.
> Any place where you turn but might have gone on,
> all possibilities need you there.
> The centers of stones need your prayers.

In "A Little Gift" (*SM*, 22), Stafford uses "night" and "blackness" symbolically as synonyms for "dark":

> Fur came near, night inside it,
> four legs at a time, when the circus
> walked off the train. From cage to cage

we carried night back to the cats and poured
it into their eyes, from ours. They
lapped steadily, and the sponge of their feet
swelled into the ground. Even today
I keep that gift: I let any next thing fold
quietly into the blackness that leads
all the way inward from the hole in my eye.

"That gift" is the imagination. "Fold/ . . . into" plays upon
the etymology of the verb "imply" which would fit the main
clause almost too neatly: "I let any next thing imply/ . . . the
blackness." Like the land in "Bi-focal," "any next thing" in
the world has a "blackness" that is "inward," a darkness that
is deep.

"Deep" and "dark" often occur together in a Stafford
poem, for example in the second stanza of "Back Home" (RY,
7): "In the maples an insect sang/ insane for hours about how
deep the dark was." As in "Bi-focal," "deep" and "dark" here
comprise a symbolic shorthand. On the symbolic level, "how
deep the dark was" suggests "how real, how imminent was the
invisible, the imaginary."

Another good example of Stafford's metaphorical use of
"deep" and "dark" (and his distance metaphor) is his poem,
"In the Deep Channel" (WOYC, 13; RY, 42). The poem's
third line, "sometimes up out of deep water," could be a deliberate echo of the first line of "Bi-focal," "Sometimes up out
of this land." Both poems imagine a consciousness in Nature;
but "In the Deep Channel" expresses none of that sense of
kinship with Nature found in "Bi-focal." It reads:

Setting a trotline after sundown
if we went far enough away in the night
sometimes up out of deep water
would come a secret-headed channel cat,

Eyes that were still eyes in the rush of darkness,
flowing feelers noncommittal and black,
and hidden in the fins those rasping bone daggers,
with one spiking upward on its back.

Bi-focal
13

We would come at daylight and find the line sag,
the fishbelly gleam and the rush on the tether:
to feel the swerve and the deep current
which tugged at the tree roots below the river.

This is one of Stafford's finest poems, uncommonly rich in
concrete detail. Like Wordsworth's "spots of time," it describes
a vivid experience of Nature but a strangely resonant one that
portends more than its surface meaning. The words "deep" and
"darkness" have, in context, a literal significance; yet the line
"Eyes that were still eyes in the rush of darkness" gives the
"darkness" an eerie, sentient aspect, for in his use of "still,"
Stafford displays one of his most characteristic devices. "Still"
has a double meaning. If one takes it as an adverb, then Stafford means that, even though it is dark, the "channel cat" can
see. But if one takes "still" as an adjective, then the poem's fifth
line suggests that the "darkness" is watching us: the eyes are
"still" because they do not blink; they are fixed on us in one,
long gaze which, if we take the adjective "still" in its Anglo-
Saxon sense, is eternal.

The syntax of the poem's first sentence is also deliberately
ambiguous. The eyes are not necessarily the eyes of the fish;
they may have come up along with the fish. Since Stafford does
not specify how many eyes there are, the repetition of "eyes"
suggests that the darkness is filled with eyes. The phrase
"secret-headed" in the fourth line contributes to the poem's
eerie quality. The suffix "-headed" also has two possible meanings. It can refer to the head of the fish; it can refer to the
direction in which the fish is "headed," which is "secret" both
in the modern sense of being unfathomable and in the Latin
sense that it is "set apart"—in this case, set apart from human
concerns. The channel cat's secrecy here conveys a more pronounced sense of Nature's otherness than one finds in "Bi-
focal." The dominant feeling of "In the Deep Channel" is close
to fear. The poem's sense of Nature's otherness is reinforced
by the word "noncommittal" in the sixth line. The degree of
difference which Stafford here feels between himself and the

natural world is relatively great. It is expressed by the word "far" in the second line: "if we went far enough away in the night." Although the line has a literal meaning in context, on the symbolic level it suggests: "if we imagined a dramatic enough difference between ourselves and the natural world."

A second metaphor which Stafford employs to express the otherness of Nature ("the world") is the word "God." For example, the poem "Sophocles Says" (*RY*, 76) begins:

> History is a story God is telling
> by means of hidden meanings written closely
> inside the skins of things. . . .

These lines might easily have been incorporated in "Bi-focal." The fact that the world's "hidden meanings" are "stories" and are "written" echoes Stafford's metaphor of a "legend" in "Bi-focal." The word "inside" echoes "deep." "Skins" echoes "surface." That which is "deep" is "hidden" because it is under the surface, "inside the skins of things." Since it cannot be visualized, it can only be imagined. "God" is roughly equivalent to "world" in "Bi-focal": the world legends; God writes.

"God," as Stafford uses the term, does not carry any orthodox religious associations. In an interview with Lewis Turco and Gregory Fitz Gerald published in *Prairie Schooner*, Stafford discussed his use of "God":

> *Fitz Gerald:* Why is it then that the concept of "God" and the word itself come up in your poetry?
> *Stafford:* Does it come up so often? If so, it could be because I'm slovenly and can't really get it all said, so I just decide to short circuit this way. I don't wish to deny religion, or a religious feeling, but neither do I seek it.
> *Turco:* You want to find what's there, right?
> *Stafford:* Yes.
> *Fitz Gerald:* Then the terminology of religion becomes sort of a metaphor.
> *Stafford:* That may be as good a way as any to put it.[1]

In the *Courier* interview, Stafford also had this to say about religious orthodoxy: "I have been identified sometimes as a religious poet or a writer of religious poems. And that seems all right to me. On the other hand, if I try to be as much on the level as possible, I have to say that orthodoxy of any kind is something that I just don't have any kind of feeling about at all. I don't even feel enough committed to deny it. . . ."[2]

The principal difference between "world" and "God" as Stafford employs these words is that whereas "world" represents Nature in a rather neutral, inert aspect, "God" represents Nature when it assumes an awesomely other aspect. For example, "The Tillamook Burn" (*TTD*, 28) begins: "These mountains have heard God;/ they burned for weeks. He spoke/ in a tongue of flame from sawmill trash/ and you can read His word down to the rock."

In "Walking the Wilderness" (*RY*, 58–59), the last section of a series called "Following the *Markings* of Dag Hammarskjöld," God is associated with all those aspects of Nature's otherness—storms, cold, winter, and death—most awful and most ultimately opposed to human interests. The first of the poem's three stanzas begins:

> God is never sure He has found
> the right grass. It never forgets Him.
> My mother in a dream dreamed
> this place, where storms drown
> down or where God makes it arch to mountains,
> flood with winter, stare upward at His
> eye that freezes people, His zero breath
> their death. . . .

The dream which "mother . . . dreamed" is her life. "This place" is the world. "His [God's] eye" is the sky. It is "God" who "makes it [the world] . . . flood with winter." The coldness of winter and of death is "His . . . breath." Yet when, in the next stanza, Stafford addresses the wintry otherness of his mother's dream, he does not address it as "God"; he merely addresses the sky: "Hear me, full sky." "God" and "sky" are interchangeable terms for Nature in its uncontrollable aspect. The second stanza ends:

> my mother in the dream dreamed
> even deeper: people drowned awake,
> each one staring, alone, pitiable,
> come to all at once in that
> dream, welcomed the more, the more
> they trembled. God never notices opposition;
> the deep of that dream always waits.

No matter how much "people" fear death, they will die ("drown"), because "God never notices opposition."

The poem's last stanza associates death with all the wintriest aspects of God and otherness:

> Snowflake designs lock; they clasp in the sky,
> hold their patterns one by one, down,
> spasms of loneliness, each one God's answer.
> Warm human representatives may vote and
> manage man; but last the blizzard will dignify
> the walker, the storm hack trees to cyclone
> groves, he catch the snow, his brave eye
> become command, the whole night howl against
> his ear, till found by dawn he
> reach out to God no trembling hand.

People die, one by one, like snowflakes. Each individual human being is like an individual snowflake with that unique pattern it holds. Stafford's death-as-drowning metaphor is continued here. When we die, we enter the ground as snowflakes do; we go deep. "Found by dawn" echoes "drowned awake" in the preceding stanza. "His brave eye [the eye of the "walker," not God's eye, since "his" is not capitalized]/ become command," relies partly on the Latin sense of "command" and echoes the curious use of "command" in Stafford's poem "Tornado" (*TTD*, 25), where he refers to the tornado as "Command": "Then Command/ moved away again." When we die we are put into the hands of God—the otherness we always feared— we "become" the other.

The implicit metaphor upon which "Walking the Wilderness" is based surfaces in the lines "Warm human representatives may vote and/ manage man; but last the blizzard will dignify/ the walker." If what is "human" is "warm" and "manage[able]," then that which is other is cold and uncontrollable. Etymologically, "human" suggests earth; the blizzard is unearthly, it comes from the air, from the sky which is God's "eye that freezes people." *Coldness* is thus, like distance, a metaphor by which Stafford measures his sense of Nature's otherness. The cold aspect of the world is its threatening aspect, threatening because it is indifferent to human life. In Stafford's poems, "cold" assumes this figurative meaning most obviously when it is used as a noun with the definite article, for example in the first line of "Owl" (*SM*, 57) which reads, "An owl—the cold with eyes—" or in the first stanza of "Spectator" (*A*, 66):

> Treat the world as if it really existed.
> Feel in the cold what hoods a mountain—
> it is not your own cold, but the world's.
> Distribute for the multitude this local discovery.

or at the end of "This Book" (*A*, ix):

> Quiet as all books, I wait, and promise
> we'll watch the night: you turn a page;
> winter misses a stride. You see
> the reason for time, for everything in the sky.
> And into your eyes I climb, on the strongest
> thread in the world, weaving the dark and the cold.

The "I" speaking above is "This Book" of the poem's title. "You" is the reader. "Weaving the dark and the cold," translated on its symbolic level, suggests "imagining the other."

Just as "night" is one of Stafford's equivalent metaphors for "dark"—for the invisible—so are "winter" and "north" equivalent counters for "cold." A good example of Stafford's symbolic use of "the North" is his poem "Bring the North" (*SM*, 41–42):

> Mushroom, Soft Ear, Old Memory,
> Root Come to Tell the Air:
> bring the Forest Floor along
> the valley; bring all that comes
> blue into passes, long shores
> around a lake, talk, talk, talk,
> miles, then deep. Bring that story.
>
> . . . .
>
> Mushroom, Soft Ear, Memory,
> attend what is.
> Bring the North.

The sentence "Bring the North" parallels "Bring that story" in the first stanza, and "what is" points back to "deep" in the seventh line: the world's legend ("that story") is "deep" ("what is"), a cold and inexorable Other ("the North").

A poem which perhaps best exemplifies Stafford's symbolic use of "cold," "God," "winter," and the distance-metaphor is "Montana Eclogue" (*A*, 28–30). The poem is set in autumn. Stafford invites us all, "we who have stopped indoors," who "forget how storms come," to imagine winter flooding into the Montana high country. The second section begins: "Far from where we are, air owns those ranches/ our trees hardly hear of, open places/ braced against cold hills. . . ." Although in context "Far" has a literal significance, Stafford is also consciously using it as a metaphor for "different," to express his sense of Nature's extreme otherness.

In the second stanza of the second section he explicitly associates distance ("Up there") and cold "air" with the noun "other":

> Up there, air like an axe chops, near timberline,
> the clear-cut miles the marmots own. We
> try to know, all deep, all sharp, even while
> busy here, that other: gripped in a job,
> aimed steady at a page, or riffled by distractions,
> we break into that world of the farthest coat—air.

In the second stanza of the poem's third and last section, Stafford addresses the reader. As in "Spectator" but here more sternly, he counsels awe and humility in the face of Nature's implacable otherness:

> *Citizen, step back from the fire and let night*
> *have your head: suddenly you more than hear*
> *what is true so abruptly that God is cold:—*
> *winter is here. What no one saw, has*
> *come. Then everything the sun approved could*
> *really fail? Shed from your back, the years*
> *fall one by one, and nothing that comes*
> *will be your fault. You breathe a few breaths*
> *free at the thought: things can come so great*
> *that your part is too small to count,*
> *if winter can come.*

"God is cold" is simply a rephrasing of "God never notices opposition." God—the world (Nature) in its uncontrollable aspect—is other to such a degree that it can only be imagined; one must "let night have" his head.

As the use of "Far" in "Montana Eclogue" and the use of "near" in "Bi-focal" suggest, Stafford's metaphor of distance as a measure of the world's imagined otherness often determines the quality of his vision in a given poem. Distance—a dramatic opposition between the walker and the world—is what, time and again, supplies the imaginative energy for a Stafford poem. The tension between the two sides of this opposition activates his poetic imagination. The distance metaphor is thus related to the darkness metaphor. Distance, whether it be explicitly presented in a poem or left implicit, is a *precondition* for darkness —for the possibility of something invisible in the world which will, because it is invisible, invite the imagination into action.

When the distance between the walker and the world is small—when the world is "near" as it is in "Bi-focal"—the walker is confronted with the visible surface of the world. What is underneath that surface, "inside the skins of things," is invisible. Thus the walker imagines a darkness under the "surface."

In "Montana Eclogue," on the other hand, Stafford is imagining a place "Far from where we are," a place which is invisible because its surface is not actually present. "Darkness" (*"Let night have your head"*) is thus manifested in the walker rather than projected into the world. The opening stanza of "Where We Are" (*A*, 70), for example, describes how the spectacle of distant mountain ranges—the obscurity lent by distance—releases the walker's imagination:

> Much travel moves mountains large
> in your eyes—and then inside,
> where those mountains climb the Everest
> of all thought—tomorrows and maybes—
> where expeditions often get lost.

The invisible potential for "all possibilities"—"tomorrows and maybes"—is manifested "inside" the walker, as a remote, high tundra of the imagination.

In the poem "Representing Far Places" (*TTD*, 75), "Far" is a metaphor not only for "other" but for the invisible. The poem's first stanza imagines a "canoe wilderness" where "fish in the lake leap arcs of realization." The poem ends:

> Often in society when the talk turns witty
> you think of that place, and can't polarize at all;
> it would be a kind of treason. The land fans in your head
> canyon by canyon; steep roads diverge.
> Representing far places you stand in the room,
> all that you know merely a weight in the weather.
>
> It is all right to be simply the way you have to be,
> among contradictory ridges in some crescendo of knowing.

The word "far" in Stafford's poetry, particularly when it is joined with images of coldness, is often associated with death. Such an association is wholly consistent with Stafford's development of his metaphor of distance. As "Walking the Wilderness" indicates, the ultimate emblem of Nature's otherness is the certainty of human mortality. In this respect, death is "far" from where we are. One's personal death is, of course, an invisible fact, an event which he can only imagine. In this respect also, death is as "far" from the human observer as the high country of Montana imagined in "Montana Eclogue" is "Far from where we are": it is not present.

The following two poems exemplify Stafford's association of distance and coldness with human death. Both poems recall Emily Dickinson's "There's a certain Slant of light," where late afternoon winter light striking across great distances becomes a faint, ethereal portent of death. "Things We Did That Meant Something" (*TTD*, 48) begins:

> Thin as memory to a bloodhound's nose,
> being the edge of some new knowing,
> I often glance at a winter color—
> husk or stalk, a sunlight touch,
> maybe a wasp nest in the brush
> near the winter river with silt like silver.

The "winter color," like Dickinson's "Slant of light," has an oppressive aura. The poem's ending seems to allude directly to the Dickinson poem: distance—the word "far"—is in the look of death.

> "Sometime the world may be hit like this
> or I getting lost may walk toward this color
> far in old sunlight with no trace at all,
> till only the grass will know I fall."

Stafford's short poem "Long Distance" (*TTD*, 77) treats the same phenomenon: late afternoon light implies a terrible distance which leads toward an unspeakable otherness, this time the death of somebody else:

> Sometimes when you watch the fire
> ashes glow and gray
> the way the sun turned cold on spires
> in winter in the town back home
> so far away.

> Sometimes on the telephone
> the one you hear goes far
> and ghostly voices whisper in.
> You think they are from other wires.
> You think they are.

As in Stafford's poem "The Farm on the Great Plains," which begins, "A telephone line goes cold," the telephone in "Long Distance" is not only a literal one; it is also a metaphor for memory, a connection to the past. "The one you hear goes far," which echoes the "I . . . may walk . . ./ far" of "Things We Did . . . ," suggests either that the speaker anticipates the death of "the one you hear" or, if the telephone is a medium of memory, that the voice "you hear" is your memory of the voice of a person already dead. This possibility is suggested by the poem's last line, "You think they are," which, prefigured by the word "ghostly," implies that "they are [still alive in your memory]."

In the poems above, the association of distance with death presents a paradox. For death, as Stafford represents it in "Walking the Wilderness," is an ultimate absence of distance between the walker and the world. They no longer have discrete identities. The walker's "brave eye become[s] command."

The image of death as drowning, as an ultimate unity of subject and object, is a constant throughout Stafford's work. For example, in the second stanza of "Uncle George" (*RY*, 16), we find: "Trapper/ of warm sight, I plow and belong, send breath/ to be part of the day, and where it arrives/ I spend on and on, fainter and fainter/ toward ultimate identification, joining the air/ a few breaths at a time. . . ." Another example of death as "ultimate identification" is the conclusion of "Believing What I Know" (*A*, 69): "I learn from the land. Some day/ like a field I may take the next thing/ so well that whatever is will be me."

Although death as ultimate identification may seem to contradict the association of death with distance in the poems above, the two sets of images are wholly consistent; for death is the final proof of how "far," how other, the world is. When Stafford writes, "I getting lost may walk toward this ["winter"] color/ far . . . ," he is imagining himself closing the "distance" between himself and the "other" until he reaches it. When he reaches it, he will be dead; he will become it. Similarly, in "Long Distance," the line "the one you hear goes far" carries the symbolic implication, "the one you hear becomes the other."

Since distance, in a Stafford poem, is a precondition for invisibility, for a darkness that invites the imagination into action, and since death is ultimate identificaton—the absence of distance—Stafford portrays absence of imagination as a kind of Death-in-Life, through images which convey a strong sense of drowning, of suffocation in the visible.

"The Poets' Annual Indigence Report" (*TTD*, 32) is typical of the few Stafford poems that describe Death-in-Life. This poem has a bitter tone which, though it lacks Coleridge's self-pity, reminds one of "Dejection: An Ode." Stafford begins:

> Tonight beyond the determined moon,
> aloft with nothing left that is voluntary
> for delight, everything uttering hydrogen,
> your thinkers are mincing along through a hail of contingencies,
>
> While we all—floating though we are, lonesome though we are,
> lost in hydrogen—we live by seems things:

The "we" speaking refers to the "Poets" in the poem's title. These poets, with Stafford as spokesman, are addressing, in the second person, some unspecified adversary. The imagery establishes a claustral ambiance. There is no sense of distance between subject and object here, because everything in the world is bleakly identical, composed of "hydrogen"; we are all "lost in hydrogen." The world is reduced to one, bright, soulless surface which, in the third stanza, Stafford calls the "dazzle floor":

> Doing is not enough; being is not enough;
> knowing is far from enough. So we clump around, putting

feet on the dazzle floor, awaiting the real schedule
by celebrating the dazzle schedule.

The "dazzle floor" corresponds to the "surface" of the world in "Bi-focal." "Dazzle" suggests that it is bright rather than dark. The dazzle floor is thus the visible, literal set of surface appearances, of "seems things" apprehended not by the imagination but by the eye. The poem ends by identifying the adversary implied by "your thinkers" in the first stanza:

Our shadows ride over the grass, your shadows, ours:—
Rich men, wise men, be our contemporaries.

The last line is ironical. It says, in effect: "Poor men, ignorant men, admit that you are like us." Riches and wisdom are but "seems things."

As the poem's first stanza suggests, the eye is here identified with reason. "Determined," "nothing left that is voluntary," "thinkers," and "contingencies" all suggest a rational, mechanical vision of the world. Stafford's identification of the eye, of the visual, with reason, and his identification of reason with absence of imagination is his equivalent to Wordsworth's labeling "the bodily eye . . ./ The most despotic of our senses" (*Prelude* XIII, 128–129). The image of the "determined moon" suggests not only "determinism" but that the moon, like the eye, is determined to hold a despotic sway "tonight."

Throughout Stafford's work, images of the moon and moonlight are associated with absence of imagination, with the visual. Such a correspondence is consistent with his symbolism, for moonlight kills darkness and, in a peculiar way, dissolves distance, emphasizing the surfaces of objects by coating everything uniformly. The *uniformity* of moonlight was what fascinated Coleridge, who thought the unifying effect of moonlight analogous to the unifying power of the imagination. The reverse is true for Stafford: by dissolving the distinction—the distance—between himself and the world, moonlight deprives him of imagination.

Bi-focal
25

One of Stafford's more interesting poems, "A Walk in the Country" (*A*, 80–81), describes a terrifying episode with moonlight. The story begins in the second stanza:

> Out in the country once,
> walking the hollow night,
> I felt a burden of silver come:
> my back had caught moonlight
> pouring through the trees like money.
>
> That walk was late, though.
> Late, I gently came into town,
> and a terrible thing had happened:
> the world, wide, unbearably bright,
> had leaped on me. I carried mountains.
>
> .   .   .   .
>
> By dawn I felt all right;
> my hair was covered with dew;
> the light was bearable; the air
> came still and cool.
> And God had come back there
> to carry the world again.

Any possibility for darkness has been destroyed by the moon, which renders the world one "unbearably bright" surface that includes Stafford himself. Like the hydrogen in "The Poets' Annual Indigence Report," the moonlight drowns him. He experiences a kind of Death-in-Life. The line, "my back had caught moonlight" recalls the phrase "he [the walker] catch the snow" from "Walking the Wilderness." The surface of the world clings to Stafford like pale dough which, for one panic-fraught moment, he cannot shake off. Only when the world's otherness reasserts itself, when the "air" is "cool," when "God" comes back "to carry the world again," is the old distance—a felt distinction of identity between himself and the "world"—reestablished.

In Stafford's poetry, the eye is the enemy of imagination because it restricts one's vision to the visible. The ear, on the other hand, is frequently associated with the imagination. Throughout Stafford's work, whenever the exercise of the imagination is represented as a mode of perception, it is almost always auditory. The word "listening" is, as Stafford employs it, generally a metaphor for "imagining." A good example of Stafford's development of this metaphor is his poem "Listening" (*WOYC*, 16; *RY*, 27):

> My father could hear a little animal step,
> or a moth in the dark against the screen,
> and every far sound called the listening out
> into places where the rest of us had never been.
>
> More spoke to him from the soft wild night
> than came to our porch for us on the wind;
> we would watch him look up and his face go keen
> till the walls of the world flared, widened.
>
> My father heard so much that we still stand
> inviting the quiet by turning the face,
> waiting for a time when something in the night
> will touch us too from that other place.

The word "listening" in the third line is here a metaphor for "imagining," and "heard" in the third stanza is a metaphor for "imagined." "The rest of us" in the fourth line refers both to the people on "our porch" other than "My father," and suggests that portion of "us" which does not participate in "listening." The lines "More spoke to him from the soft wild night/ than came to our porch for us on the wind" also carry a double meaning: "My father" could imagine or "hear" more than "the rest of us"; what he imagined, what "spoke to him" was "more" than a "little animal step,/ or a moth . . . against the screen"—noises one would expect to hear on a summer night— more than could be rationally accounted for.

The act of "listening" is not passively receptive. It is a reciprocal transaction between the walker and the world. Whereas "every far sound called the listening out" suggests that the source of any "call" or invitation to the imagination is "out" in the natural world, "inviting the quiet" in the last stanza suggests the reverse—that the walker initiates the invitation, that the imagination is an active power rather than a receptive faculty. This paradox which figures in a number of Stafford's poems is at the heart of Stafford's theory of the imagination, and it is the theme of one of his most complicated poems, "From the Gradual Grass" (*TTD*, 76).[3] The poem, which is in three stanzas, begins:

> Imagine a voice calling,
> "There is a voice now calling,"
> or maybe a blasting cry:
> "Walls are falling!"
> as it makes walls be falling.

> Then from the gradual grass,
> too serious to be only noise—
> whatever it is grass makes,
> making words, a voice:

The paradox proposed above is similar to Coleridge's, "Oh Lady, we receive but what we give/ And in our life alone does Nature live" in "Dejection: An Ode." If we imagine a voice calling from the grass, we may actually hear a voice. The imagination is that powerful. Furthermore, once the "voice" of the imagination starts "calling,/ 'There is a voice now calling,' " the two voices become so confused that, as in the poem "Listening," it is difficult to determine where the "call" originated, to distinguish between cause and effect. Did the call originate from the grass, or did one merely pretend that it did?

In the second stanza, Stafford abruptly stops theorizing and proposes an experiment to test his hypothesis. He wants to make the "call" from the grass seem as independent as possible; the sound of grass moving in the wind is "too serious to be only noise—." It is "making words, a voice." The grass says:

> "Destruction is ending; this voice

"Is promising quiet: silence
by lasting forever grows to sound
endlessly from the world's end
promising, calling."
Imagine. *That voice is calling.*

A deliberate ambiguity is developed here. The grass itself,
which we have been invited to imagine is speaking, refers to
" 'this voice.' " Does the grass mean its own voice? Is it saying,
in effect, " '[*my*] voice/ 'Is promising quiet' "? For one pre-
carious moment, it seems so. But Stafford has already hinted,
in the line "whatever it is grass makes," that he knows as well
as we do that grass cannot make actual words. When the grass
does seem to be "making words," the words are, of course, Stafford's translation of a sound "too serious to be only noise." Had
the grass said " '*my* voice,' " or " 'I am promising quiet,' " we
would react as we would if confronted with one of Walt
Disney's talking animals: we might acquiesce in the fiction,
but we would not take it seriously. By imagining the grass
saying " 'this voice,' " Stafford deliberately confuses *his* voice
with the voice of the grass: " 'this' " can refer to either. The
effect of such ambiguity is two-fold: to remind the reader that
the words of the poem are all Stafford's; to insist also that we
must not deny the mysterious sense (which the poem evokes)
that grass *can* in some strange way seem to speak to us.

To sustain the authenticity of such a sense, Stafford's translation of the grass's speech must be absolutely plausible; other-
wise the reader will dismiss the poem as cheap sleight-of-hand.
The poem succeeds because Stafford's translation is so vague—as
vague as any message from the grass might be. The grass's
message is lowly, redundant, almost trivial. It seems to be
trying to mean something, but this meaning is either hidden or
wholly intrinsic. It is as cryptic and inexorable as the legend
in "Bi-focal."

The poem ends: "Imagine. *That voice is calling.*" We
know that Stafford is speaking here, because "Imagine" is not
in quotation marks. It directs us back to the beginning of the

poem, "Imagine a voice calling," and renders the entire poem reflexive. The poem has asked it*self* a question: Grass can seem to have a voice. Does this voice originate in Nature? Or is it merely the echo of an illusion, of a sound activated by the poem's language and broadcast by the imagination? The answer is a paradox: we receive but what we give.

A longer poem, "The Animal That Drank Up Sound" (*RY*, 78–79), develops systematically Stafford's correspondence between "sound" and the invisible, his concept of the imagination as an echo-producing power and his notion of the eye as the enemy of imagination. Stafford told me that he wrote this poem after hearing some American Indian legends, and he thought he would enjoy making up his own legend in which elements of the natural world were used as characters in a story of human significance. Like Coleridge's "Rime of the Ancient Mariner" or Wallace Stevens's "The Comedian as the Letter C," "The Animal That Drank Up Sound" is a symbolic tale whose theme is the poetic imagination. It begins:

> One day across the lake where echoes come now
> an animal that needed sound came down. He gazed
> enormously, and instead of making any, he took
> away from, sound: the lake and all the land
> went dumb. A fish that jumped went back like a knife,
> and the water died. In all the wilderness around he
> drained the rustle from the leaves into the mountainside

The animal has come down to the lake because it needs to drink "sound." Instead of making sound, which would produce echoes, the animal "gazed/ enormously": the animal drinks in everything with its eye. The animal continues to drink "till winter," until there is no sound left in the world. Then the animal begins to "starve." The moon, always a killer of imagination, rises and holds a despotic reign over the world:

> When the moon drifted over that night the whole world lay
> just like the moon, shining back that still
> silver, and the moon saw its own animal dead
> on the snow. . . .

The animal has achieved a kind of Death-in-Life. The moon is "delighted": "The moon/ owned the earth its animal had faithfully explored." But, as the grass says in "From the Gradual Grass," "silence/ by lasting forever grows to sound." The story has a happy ending:

> But on the north side of a mountain, deep in some rocks,
> a cricket slept. It had been hiding when that animal
> passed, and as spring came again this cricket waited,
> afraid to crawl out into the heavy stillness.
> Think how deep the cricket felt, lost there
> in such a silence—the grass, the leaves, the water,
> the stilled animals all depending on such a little
> thing. But softly it tried—"Cricket!"—and back like a river
> from that one act flowed the kind of world we know,
> first whisperings, then moves in the grass and leaves;

"The Animal That Drank Up Sound" is best interpreted if we simply substitute "eye" for "animal." The passage "He gazed/ enormously, and . . . took/ away from sound" then assumes a fairly obvious meaning. The eye, by definition, rules out all the invisible possibilities, all "sound," upon which the imagination depends.

The cricket, on the other hand, is the poetic imagination, which spontaneously reasserts itself to renovate the world. It is all those possibilities which the imagination can construe about whatever is invisible. The eye, which scans only literal surface appearances, cannot perceive the cricket hidden *in* the rocks; the eye passes over it. As Stafford expresses this: "It [the cricket] had been hiding when that animal/ passed." But, although the "sound" which the cricket makes may *appear* to originate from the rocks, it is actually the echo of a "sound" projected by the human imagination into the dark interior of the world, an echo which, although completely dependent upon a prior "sound," is so convincing that we suspend disbelief and "listen," imagine a voice calling from the rocks. The poem's last line cryptically presents the paradox: "It [the cricket] listens now, and practices at night." When the cricket calls

" 'Cricket!' " the world, in auditory terms, "legends itself deep"; but it is a legend attributed to the world by Stafford's imagination.

𝕮̃he 𝕰arth Says--

The legend which Stafford imagines that "God is telling" is deep but dark, true but invisible. Its meanings are "hidden," "written closely inside the skins of things." What meanings, then, does Stafford imagine in the world's story? In the third and fourth stanzas of "Late Thinker" (*TTD*, 87–88), he asks himself the same question:

> he [the poet] questions those pale towns,
> turns to those haggard lands.
> Where are the wrongs men have done?
> He holds out calloused hands
> toward that landscape of justice.
>
> He counts each daily meeting [with Nature],
> the stare of its blind meaning,
> and maintains an autumn allegiance,
> but what can he lean toward?

The "meaning" of the world's legend is "blind"—invisible both because it is imagined and because it cannot be interpreted. Yet the natural landscape exhibits, for Stafford, a "justice." In its Latin sense, the word "just" means "fitting." "Justice," then, suggests fittingness. Although the meaning of natural history is "blind," Stafford imagines, among the elements of the natural world, a fittingness, a propriety which stands as an implicit lesson for human beings to follow.

In a short essay, "At Home On Earth," in the *Hudson Review*, Stafford attributes such a propriety to "organic processes":

> Outside our councils the world is beginning to speak. It will never finish; no person can interpret it fully. But it is there, and that it has something urgent to say, we are beginning to be convinced. . . .
>
> In the world where what is outside man extends into mystery, awe, worship, respect, reverence—poetry, the stance that accepts, may be salvational. The psyche may depend upon limitation, recurrence, stability, as do organic processes. The disruption of feeling for purposes of gain may endanger a balance the individual has to have. . . .[1]

As the passage above indicates, the "justice" which Stafford sees in the natural landscape is associated with the "limitation, recurrence, stability" of "organic processes." Such a justice may stand as an implicit model for human behavior; but, as Stafford is careful to point out, the validity of this model must be taken on faith, through the "stance that accepts" all possibilities. Nevertheless, the model may be "salvational." The human species may be able, by adopting it on faith, to save itself.

The imaginative use of Nature as an emblem of propriety, as a model for "salvation," is a major theme in Stafford's poetry. A good example of his treatment of this theme is his poem "In Response to a Question" (*TTD*, 33):

> The earth says have a place, be what that place
> requires; hear the sound the birds imply
> and see as deep as ridges go behind
> each other. (Some people call their scenery flat,
> their only picture framed by what they know:
> I think around them rise a riches and a loss
> too equal for their chart—but absolutely tall.)
>
> The earth says every summer have a ranch
> that's minimum: one tree, one well, a landscape

that proclaims a universe—sermon
of the hills, hallelujah mountain,
highway guided by the way the world is tilted,
reduplication of mirage, flat evening:
a kind of ritual for the wavering.

The earth says where you live wear the kind
of color that your life is (gray shirt for me)
and by listening with the same bowed head that sings
draw all into one song, join
the sparrow on the lawn, and row that easy
way, the rage without met by the wings
within that guide you anywhere the wind blows.

Listening, I think that's what the earth says.

The form of this poem resembles "From the Gradual
Grass." In attributing words to the earth, both poems establish
a deliberate confusion between Stafford's voice and what "the
earth says." Both poems thus posit the same relation between
the human imagination and the world. The "I" in the first
stanza's penultimate line, although it could, syntactically, refer
to "the earth" ("The earth says . . . : I think"), actually refers to
the poet. Such deliberate confusion of voice is resolved in the
poem's last line. Like the end of "From the Gradual Grass,"
"Listening, I think that's what the earth says" insists unequiv-
ocally that "I" is the poet and that what "the earth says" is
imagined. Implicit in both poems is Stafford's theory of the
imagination as an echo-producing power. Here the echo metaphor is buried in the word "requires," which is used here as
"call" is used in "From the Gradual Grass." If "requires" is
taken in its Latin sense, "be what that place/ requires" implies
that what the "earth says" is whatever is asked of it, whatever
the human imagination wishes it to say. If "requires" is taken
in its modern sense of "demands," then the line assumes another
meaning: whatever one's "place" demands of him is whatever
he imagines.

The word "place" in the first line introduces one of the

most important metaphors in Stafford's poetry, one which is intimately related to the distance metaphor. If differences of identity are measured in terms of distance, then, implicit *in* the distance metaphor is the correspondence of *place* to identity; for the very concept of distance presupposes two discrete points or "places." It is in this sense that the word "place" is used in the last line of "Listening": "that other place [Nature]" is a metaphor for "that different identity." Generally, then, throughout Stafford's work, the noun "place" is a concrete way of expressing the abstract concept of particularness or identity. In the poem "Earth Dweller" (*A*, 79), for example, the passage, "If I have not found the right place/ teach me," uses "place" in this sense.

Sometimes, as in the following passage from "Allegiances" (*A*, 77), although the word "place" does not occur, the concept of "place" is implicit: "It is time . . ./ . . . for all of us common ones/ to locate ourselves by the real things/ we live by." To "locate ourselves" is "to find a place for ourselves." As this passage suggests, "place" is not a static concept. We "locate ourselves" *by* a process.

In "Love the Butcher Bird Lurks Everywhere" (*TTD*, 62), Stafford refers to "willows" which "do tricks to find an exact place in the wind:/ resolution steady, bent to be true." The "exact place" or identity of "willows" is defined through their behavior, by their "bent." The "place" of *any* element in the world, be it human or natural, is defined, for Stafford, through *process*. In "In Response to a Question" (*TTD*, 33), for example, "place" is represented as a set of activities expressed through *verbs*: "be what that place/ requires"; "hear the sound"; "see as deep"; "have a ranch"; "wear the kind of color"; etc. The form of the poem is one of iterated exhortation. Stafford is prescribing those processes which, he believes, define the ideal "place" of both the human species and the human individual with respect to Nature. Implicit throughout the poem is his faith in the justice of the natural world as a model for human activity or process. "Hear the sound the birds imply" suggests, in context, that "birds," that all elements of the natural world, have an ideal "place"; but it is a place which we can only "hear"—an ideal which can only be imagined. The importance of imagination as a way of faith is reinforced by the passage, "and see as deep as ridges go behind/ each other." For the human being to "have a place" he must rely on faith, must "see" the invisible.

The second stanza of "In Response" appeals more explicitly to the natural world as a model of justice. "A ranch that's minimum" echoes Thoreau's concept of economy. The minimum is no more than is necessary. The "minimum" as a metaphor for an ideal economy of process is one which Stafford uses elsewhere, for example in "And That Picnic at Zigzag" (*A*, 41): "Tea at a campfire,/ talk under the wind—/ that was minimum living, Friend." In the second stanza of "Ice-fishing" (*WOYC*, 49; *RY*, 67), Stafford imagines an ideal "minimum" in natural process: "When the night comes I plunge my hand/ where the string of fish know their share/ of the minimum."

As the word "night" in the passage above indicates, Stafford's concept of the "minimum" is wholly imagined. It is not, as Thoreau's concept of economy is, based upon minute, empirical observation. Stafford admitted to me that he is "always conscious of" Thoreau. But he is not, as Thoreau was, a naturalist. His vision of an ideal "justice" in the natural world conspicuously lacks Thoreau's authority.

"A ranch that's minimum" carries a second connotation which depends upon the etymological relationship between "ranch" and "rank." "Have a ranch that's minimum" carries the distinct suggestion, "have a rank that's low." Stafford believes that the proper human position with respect to the world is humble. Nevertheless, no matter how austere, how "minimum" one's ranch, his imagination can create, from one "landscape," a "universe" and discover a "sermon" in the "hills." "Hallelujah mountain" recalls "Walking the Wilderness": "God makes it arch to mountains," which suggests the uncontrollable aspect of Nature (God). "Highway guided by the way the world is tilted" counsels a posture of submission to the uncontrollable. The stanza's last two lines echo "Some people call their scenery flat,/ their only picture framed by what they know" in the first stanza. The awe enforced upon the walker by the scale and otherness of Nature cannot be continuously borne. "Reduplication of mirage" implies "redoubling" of the mirage of surface appearances, of seems things, as an antidote to fear.[2]

The third stanza begins by refining, slightly, the concept of the "minimum" introduced in the second stanza, and again appeals implicitly to the natural world as a model for human propriety. "Wear the kind/ of color that your life is (gray shirt for me)" seems to allude directly to Thoreau's philosophy of clothing:

> If you have any enterprise before you, try it in your old clothes. All men want, not something to *do with*, but something to *do,* or rather something to *be.* Perhaps we should never procure a new suit, however ragged or dirty the old, until we have so conducted, so enterprised or sailed in some way, that we feel like new men in the old, . . . Otherwise we shall be found sailing under false colors, and be inevitably cashiered at last by our own opinion, as well as that of mankind.
>
> *(Walden,* I)

The stanza's next three lines reiterate the primacy of imagination in constructing the world. The stanza ends: ". . . and row that easy/ way, the rage without met by the wings/ within that guide you anywhere the wind blows." The wind image here recalls the willows which "do tricks to find an exact place in the wind." The "easy way" for a human being to "have a place" is, as the willows do, to "find" it—through faith in "the wings within," to let oneself be "guided" by an uncontrollable but just process which is invisible. As Stafford expresses this faith in "Parentage" *(TTD,* 20): "I'd just as soon be pushed by events to where I belong."

"In Response to a Question" presents, rather cryptically, a

major portion of Stafford's vision—his theory of the imagination, his faith in the justice of Nature as a model for human behavior and some of the inferences he draws from this model: that there is an ideal human "place" in the world, that this "place" is a humble one, that this "place" is defined through process, that the way to find this "place" is to live economically and, through faith in "the wings/ within," be "guided."

Stafford's vision of an ideal human "place" defined through just process manifests itself both in poems of social criticism and in poems about his personal movement to "find an exact place" where "I belong." His poems of social criticism are usually pronounced from a stance of moral authority. Human activities which do not cohere to his model of natural justice—which do not imitate natural process—Stafford attacks for their perversity. A good example of a Stafford poem which criticizes human society for violation of the "minimum" is "Two Evenings" (*WOYC*, 48), which ends: "Counting the secretaries coming out of a building/ there were more people than purposes./ We stared at the sidewalk looking for ourselves,/ like antelope fading into the evening."

Another example is the fifth section of "The Move to California" (*WOYC*, 40; *RY*, 74), a poem which describes Stafford's move, in 1955, from Manchester College in Indiana to San Jose State College. The fifth section, "Along Highway 40," reads:

> Those who wear green glasses through Nevada
> travel a ghastly road in unbelievable cars
> and lose pale dollars
> under violet hoods when they park at gambling houses.
>
> I saw those martyrs—all sure of their cars in the open
> and always believers in any handle they pulled—
> wracked on an invisible cross
> and staring at a green table.
>
> While the stars were watching
> I crossed the Sierras in my old Dodge

letting the speedometer measure God's kindness,
and slept in the wilderness on the hard ground.

"Green glasses" and "violet hoods" in the first stanza echo
"wear the kind/ of color that your life is" in "In Response."
They are emblems of human perversity. The word "martyrs"
in the second stanza is meant ironically. Whereas these "martyrs" are "believers in any handle," Stafford is a believer in
"God's kindness," in gravity. The martyrs are "sure of their
cars," sure of what is man-made. Stafford lets *his* "speedometer
measure God's kindness"; he derives his momentum *from*
Nature, by coasting in accordance with natural forces. The
martyrs depend on "handles" for speed; they accelerate, attempt
to overcome "God's kindness."

Stafford's social criticism is usually more general than the
poems above might indicate. It is leveled against human denial
of process. The primary form of perversity which Stafford criticizes is pride, and the primary symptom of human pride is the
refusal to be "guided by the wings/ within," by process. The
most perverse and, perhaps, the most dangerous men, Stafford
believes, are men who, believing in *reason*, impose their own
plans upon the world, men who, like the "thinkers" in "The
Poets' Annual Indigence Report," are "mincing along through
a hail of contingencies." Stafford's brief poem, "An Epiphany"
(*A*, 54), for example, begins: "You thinkers, prisoners of what
will work:/ a dog ran by me in the street one night,/ its path
met by its feet in quick unthought." Implicit in these lines is
Stafford's assumption that the dog is following the right path
and his opinion that "unthought" is the easiest way to find a
right "path."

Stafford's notion of "thinkers" as "prisoners" recurs in the
middle stanza of "Freedom" (*SM*, 68):

No leader is free; no follower is free—
the rest of us can often be free.
Most of the world are living by

> creeds too odd, chancy, and habit-forming
> to be worth arguing about by reason.

This stanza, particularly in the second line, is heavily ironical. The "rest of us" may not exist. If they do, "often" may mean either seldom or never. These ironies undercut the shrillness of "Most of the world" and make the last two lines suggest their opposite meaning: "Most of the world" are living by creeds which seem to them so normal, so self-evident, and so immutable that they regard their creeds as virtually synonymous with "reason" itself. Here, as in "An Epiphany," Stafford's tone is mocking. "It Is the Time You Think" (*WOYC*, 56), on the other hand, although its beginning resembles the beginning of "An Epiphany," is not funny. It is about the "peninsula of fear" upon which "I stand" during the Cold War: "Deaf to process, alive only to ends,/ such are the thinkers around me, the logical ones—." The arrogant use of reason as a guide to achieve "ends" is a violation of process, perverse because, in the natural world—Stafford's model of justice—process is an end in itself.

Stafford's most common image for process is the image of a "path." This metaphor interlocks closely with both his metaphors of distance and place. "Place" is identity. Differences of identity are measured in terms of a physical distance between places. Since identity is defined through process, and identity is represented as a "place," that process which determines a given identity may be regarded as a *movement toward* a "place."

If, as Stafford believes, organic processes depend on "limitation, recurrence, stability," they exhibit a definite pattern. It is in this sense that the process which defines the identity of a given element of the natural world is, like the world's legend as represented in "Bi-focal," prescribed. The metaphor of "path" for process is thus particularly appropriate, because "path" carries the connotation of prescription, of pattern: a path is a set of marks which one *follows*. This is how "path" is used in the beginning of "An Epiphany": the dog's "path" is its natural "bent" to be true, its prescribed potential as an organism—a potential which is realized through perfection of the processes for which it is adapted. But, as "quick unthought" suggests, the dog cannot see the "path" which it is following. It blindly acts according to its natural bent.

Since "place" is defined through process, it is not static. While an organism is alive and manifesting the process prescribed for it, its "place" is never fully realized. Only when it dies—when its path is ended and thus complete—does its ideal "place" assume a closed and ultimate definition: the configuration of the path which it left behind it, the sum of that organism's gestures, the visible and outward "legend" of its prescribed, inner bent. One suspects that it is the "recurrence" of organic processes in Nature which, for Stafford, suggests a "justice" in the natural landscape. We recall the opening lines of "Walking the Wilderness": "God is never sure he has found the right grass." The fact that "grass" repeatedly manifests the same identity suggests, for Stafford, that grass has an ideal "place."

In Stafford's opinion, the most disastrous consequence of human pride in reason and denial of process is human warfare.[3] His poem "Watching the Jet Planes Dive" (*WYOC*, 37) is built around the metaphor of a path:

> We must go back and find a trail on the ground
> back of the forest and mountain on the slow land;
> we must begin to circle on the intricate sod.
> By such wild beginnings without help we may find
> the small trail on through the buffalo-bean vines.
>
> We must go back with noses and the palms of our hands,
> and climb over the map in far places, everywhere,
> and lie down whenever there is doubt and sleep there.
> If roads are unconnected we must make a path,
> no matter how far it is, or how lowly we arrive.
>
> We must find something forgotten by everyone alive,
> and make some fabulous gesture when the sun goes down
> as they do by custom in little Mexico towns

where they crawl for some ritual up a rocky steep.
The jet planes dive; we must travel on our knees.

The form of this poem is an iterated chant. Its movement describes a series of slow circles, a shamanistic dance. "We" are the tribe, and Stafford is the shaman. At the poem's center is the metaphor of path as process. A "trail" must be "found" "on the slow land" but "without help" and "in far places." "Far" here carries its usual symbolic level of "other"; "far places" is Stafford's symbolic shorthand for "other identities," "the slow land" of Nature. "Without help" suggests "without" the "help" of reason, without artificial guides. "We must make a path,/ no matter how far it is," means, on the symbolic level, we must acquiesce in a process and live by it no matter how different ("far") it is from the way we have been living. "We must find something forgotten by everyone alive" implies that the ideal "path" we must "find" is prescribed but has been "forgotten" both in the sense that we have strayed from it and in the sense that the prescribed path of an organism is one which it follows blindly. "And make some fabulous gesture when the sun goes down" reminds us that to accept the possibility of such a "path" involves an act of faith, of the imagination. The poem's last line envisions "jet planes" as an emblem of perverse human pride. Our right path is "lowly." Human beings belong on the ground, not in the air.

Another example of Stafford's use of the natural world as a model for human behavior and a touchstone for social criticism is his poem "At the Bomb Testing Site" (*WOYC*, 31; *RY*, 32):

> At noon in the desert a panting lizard
> waited for history, its elbows tense,
> watching the curve of a particular road
> as if something might happen.
>
> It was looking for something farther off
> than people could see, an important scene
> acted in stone for little selves
> at the flute end of consequences.

The Earth Says—

> There was just a continent without much on it
> under a sky that never cared less.
> Ready for a change, the elbows waited.
> The hands gripped hard on the desert.

"History" in the second line recalls the beginning of "Sophocles Says" (*RY*, 76): "History is a story God is telling,/ by means of hidden meanings written closely/ inside the skins of things." It is the prescribed "path" of "things" both human and natural. "Waited for history" is bitterly ironical. The "lizard" is about to be destroyed by a turn in human history. The apparent perversity of human history may be incompatible with natural history.

"Road," in the third line, implies a path, a process. The lizard, an emblem of natural propriety, is blindly following its just path, its "particular road." Unlike human history, the lizard's path is in harmony with natural history, which is "farther off than people could see"—more different, more "other" than people could imagine. Natural history is also more "important" than human history, both because its scale is transcendent and because its meaning is "imported"; it is other. "Scene/ acted" in the second stanza continues an implicit comparison between human history and natural history. The "important" scenes are "acted in stone for little selves" like the lizard, not for men, who are too proud to see themselves as the "little selves" they are.

"Our City Is Guarded by Automatic Rockets" (*RY*, 20), focuses upon human perversity as a denial of process. The poem, which is in three stanzas, begins:

> Breaking every law except the one
> for Go, rolling its porpoise way, the rocket
> staggers on its course; its feelers lock
> a stranglehold ahead; and—rocking—finders
> whispering "Target, Target," back and forth,
> relocating all its meaning in the dark,
> it freezes on the final stage. . . .

The rocket is an emblem of human perversity, of behavior that is "deaf to process, alive only to ends." Such behavior "break[s] every law."

The poem's second section appeals to natural justice as a possible human model:

> Bough touching bough, touching . . . till the shore,
> a lake, an undecided river, and a lake again
> saddling the divide: a world that won't be wise
> and let alone, but instead is found outside
> by little channels, linked by chance, not stern;
> and then when once we're sure we hear a guide
> it fades away toward the opposite end of the road
> from home—the world goes wrong in order to have revenge.
> Our lives are an amnesty given us.

The image of a "lake" as "an undecided river" is an emblem of natural process. In contrast to the rocket, water, by *following* "every law," although it may appear "undecided," finds its proper destination. In the third line, "a world" refers both to the human and the natural world. The natural world— one which will not be "wise"—will not *be* "let alone" by the human world. "Wise" is meant ironically here, as it is in "The Poets' Annual Indigence Report" ("Rich men, wise men, . . ."). Stafford distrusts the vanity of purported human wisdom.[4] Elements of the natural world behave justly because they do not pretend to wisdom. Nature, the world "found outside," is "not stern" as the rocket is. If "world" in the third line refers to the *human* world, then the sense of the passage is that humanity will not exhibit the true wisdom of the natural world, which is to "let alone." The stanza's last two lines have a double meaning. If "revenge" is taken in its Latin sense, then "the world goes wrong in order to have revenge" echoes the image of the "undecided river" above. Water finds its ultimate and proper destination through a kind of trial-and-error process; Nature corrects itself. "Revenge" is vindication. "Our lives are an amnesty given us" then employs the Greek sense of "amnesty" as "forgetfulness of wrong." Apparent human folly such as war may be self-correcting—a part of a process or path by which the human species moves toward its ultimate destination, its ideal place." Human amnesty thus allows the species, like water, to go wrong in order to correct itself. This faint note of hope is outweighed by the lines' second possible interpretation—that for engaging in the folly of war, humanity will suffer a revenge which it deserves, and that even now we are fortunate to be alive.

In the third stanza, Stafford imagines himself as a wildcat who will "spit/ life, at the end of any trail where I smell any hunter,/ because I think our story should not end—/ or go on in the dark with nobody listening." "Our story" comprehends both human and natural history. This story, the world's legend, could "go on" without its human strand; but it is "our" story because, as the word "listening" suggests, we are imagining it; we have, figuratively, created it.

Another example of Stafford's use of a natural model for social criticism is "Deerslayer's Campfire Talk" (*A*, 74), which begins:

> At thousands of places on any
> mountain, exact rock faces lean
> a strong-corner slant, balanced:
> the whole country stays by such dependable
> sets and shoulders—which endure unnoted.
>   Bend after bend the river washes
> its hands, never neglecting to kiss
> every drop to every other—but that
> is a small thing, not important.
>   Tribes, or any traveling people,
> will have some who stoke the fire
> or carry the needed supplies—but
> they take few great positions; hardly
> anyone cares about them.

The "whole country" has a double meaning: the natural land-scape and the United States. The elements that keep Nature "balanced" and "dependable" are, like the elements that keep a nation "balanced," those which "endure unnoted" but which, by carrying on the most basic activities essential to life, such as "stok[ing] the fire," move in harmony with natural process. The image of the river is an image of something so at peace with itself that all its elements routinely kiss each other.

In the second stanza, Stafford contrasts the country's "dependable" elements with its dangerous ones:

> Wherever I go they quote people
> who talk too much, the ones who
> do not care, just so they take the center
> and call the plans.

The people who "call the plans" are thinkers who are deaf to process. Their denial of process results from their pride in their "plans." The poem ends:

> . . . I favor what helps, and ordinary
> men, and that dim arch above us we seldom
> regard, and—under us—the silent,
> unnoted clasp of the rock.

The justice of natural process, against which the warlike aspect of human history may appear perverse, must, like the unnoted clasp of rock, be taken on faith; it must be imagined. Imagination may be salvational. The perverse aspect of human history, the part furthered by "thinkers" who reason with "contingencies," Stafford sees as an aspect of "the dazzle floor" of "seems things." It is false. As Stafford expresses it in "Bess" (*A*, 4): "And the great national events danced/ their grotesque, fake importance." This "dance" is the enemy of imagination, a crippling and perhaps dangerous distraction from what is "dependable" and "deep."

Stafford's poem "Evening News" (*A*, 58) proposes a scale of "depth." At one end of the scale is a television screen's thin and therefore false version of the world. Near the center of the scale is "our . . . house," which is "thick." At the "deep" end is Nature. The poem reads:

That one great window puts forth
its own scene, the whole world
alive in glass. In it a war happens,
only an eighth of an inch thick.
Some of our friends have leaped
through, disappeared, become unknown
voices and rumors of crowds.

In our thick house, every evening
I turn from that world,
and room by room I walk, to
enjoy space. At the sink I start
a faucet; water from far is
immediate on my hand. I open our
door, to check where we live.
In the yard I pray birds,
wind, unscheduled grass,
that they please help to make
everything go deep again.

"Thick house" deliberately echoes "eighth of an inch
thick" in the first stanza. "Our . . . house" is thicker than "that
world" in the television screen. "Water from far" leads Stafford's imagination out "our/ door" to Nature, which is "deep."

The poem's movement, like that of "A Walk in the Country," is from a suffocating Death-in-Life toward restoration of
"distance." Like moonlight, like the "dazzle floor" of hydrogen
in "The Poets' Annual Indigence Report," the television's despotic "scene" threatens to dissolve Stafford's identity. The
image of "our friends" who have "leaped/ through, disappeared" is an image of death-by-drowning, death as ultimate
identification with the literal—the death of imagination.

The second stanza describes the process by which Stafford
tries to disengage himself, to contract his identity into a bearable
focus with respect to the world, to reestablish that distance
which is both a precondition for invisibility—for the salvational
imagination to operate again—and the measure of his felt identity. The images here are spatial. "I walk, to/ enjoy space";

"water from far"; "where we live." The movement of the stanza is toward greater distance, toward a sense of relief at identity reaffirmed. "Space" in the fourth line leads to "far" in the fifth which evokes a renewed sense of "where we live" ("who we are"). Once we know who we are, everything can "go deep again": God will carry the world.

4 My Self Will Be the Plain

Quite often in a Stafford poem his sense of his "place" as a human individual will be expressed in terms of another metaphor, the word "home." Such a correspondence is established in Stafford's poem "In Dear Detail, by Ideal Light" (*TTD*, 91). This poem, which consists of two sections, is addressed to an unspecified "you" who, like the "Ella" in Stafford's Ella-poems, is a spirit of the past, a symbol of his nostalgic memory of his Kansas childhood and adolescence. The last two stanzas of the first section read:

> Gradually we left you there
> surrounded by the river curve
> and the held-out arms,
> elms under the streetlight.
>
> These vision emergencies come
> wherever we go—
> blind home
> coming near at unlikely places.

"Wherever we go" we carry with us a wistful ideal of "home." The source of this "vision emergency" is one's memory of his childhood home. The ideal is "blind" because it is imagined. "Unlikely places" has two levels of meaning. If we take "places" literally, then Stafford is suggesting that one's "vision emergencies" of his childhood home manifest themselves independently of his physical location. If we take "places" as a metaphor for felt identity, then "unlikely places" suggests that, although one's adult sense of identity may vary, his memory of his childhood identity is a constant.

In the second section, Stafford implies that he finds the discrepancy between his adult "place" and his memory of "home" dissatisfying in the light of his natural model:

> One's duty: to find a place
> that grows from his part of the world—
> it means leaving
> certain good people.

One's adult sense of home should grow "from his part of the world," be self-created, independent of time and place. Implicit in the word "grows" is Stafford's appeal to a natural model, to his belief in identity as defined through an organic process. The remainder of the poem describes the ideal "home" which Stafford imagines, a place where:

> . . . for the rest of the years,
> by not going there, a person could believe
> some porch looking south,
> and steady in the shade—maybe you,

Such a home is "an imagined place/ Where finally the way the world feels/ really means how things are,/ in dear detail,/ by ideal light all around us." As the phrase "ideal light" suggests, the ideal is an impossible one. Its "porch" looks "south." Stafford's imagined place does not comprehend the existence of death. If it did, the "porch" would look "north" toward the cold. This "imagined place" is a childish identity, a child's sense of home, in which the spirit of the past, "maybe you," is present and "steady in the shade." The ideal is all the more impossible because a child's sense of home is not self-created but depends upon his sense of home as a literal physical location; it does not grow "from his part of the world." "In

Dear Detail," then, proposes a nostalgic ideal which Stafford recognizes is impossible but whose impossibility points implicitly to some of the harder truths of the human position.

In Stafford's poem "The Farm on the Great Plains" (*WOYC*, 19; *RY*, 26), he contrasts his childhood memory of home to the grimmer sense of "home" he has learned to accept as an adult. When one's parents die, his childhood sense of "place" as a literal physical location can no longer be sustained. Only a memory remains, a vision emergency of "blind home." In "The Farm on the Great Plains," Stafford describes how as an adult he still involuntarily grasps at this vision emergency only to have it trickle through his fingers and his sense of "space" collapse in upon him with the realization that his parents are dead, that his "home" is "my self," which is independent of time and space. This "home" is not the impossible ideal yearned for in "In Dear Detail." It comprehends the certainty of mortality. The poem reads as follows:

> A telephone line goes cold;
> birds tread it wherever it goes.
> A farm back of a great plain
> tugs an end of the line.
>
> I call that farm every year,
> ringing it, listening, still;
> no one is home at the farm,
> the line gives only a hum.
>
> Some year I will ring the line
> on a night at last the right one,
> and with an eye tapered for braille
> from the phone on the wall
>
> I will see the tenant who waits—
> the last one left at the place;
> through the dark my braille eye
> will lovingly touch his face.
>
> "Hello, is Mother at home?"
> *No one is home today.*

My Self Will Be the Plain

"But Father—he should be there."
No one—no one is here.

"But you—are you the one . . . ?"
Then the line will be gone
because both ends will be home:
no space, no birds, no farm.

My self will be the plain,
wise as winter is gray,
pure as cold posts go
pacing toward what I know.

As in "Long Distance," the telephone is here a medium for
memory. Since Stafford's mother and father are dead, the line
along which his imagination races must extend into the "cold."
The phrase "braille eye" echoes "blind home" with a curious
accuracy.

A feeling of tense anticipation is established by "at last
the right one." The relief and eagerness of the insistent child
in Stafford increases with " 'Hello, is Mother at home?' " " 'But
Father—he should be there' " conveys a tone of dawning dis-
appointment, frustration, apprehension, which collapses in
stunned realization: "no space, no birds, no farm." "Home"
(the farm on the plain) no longer exists in "space"; home is
"my self," the place from which Stafford originated the call.

"My self will be the plain" carries two other meanings.
The "plain"—Stafford's memory of Kansas, where he grew
up—is contained within his "self." "My self" is mortal; it
"will be[come] the plain," the other. For Stafford, the death
of his parents is a convincing premonition of his own eventual
death. The remainder of the poem builds this sense of certainty
and contains, as a buried metaphor, the image of a path. The
"cold posts," like the future steps his individual path will make,
lead toward the "cold" otherness of the plain, toward "what
I know."

A more explicitly biographical poem, "Circle of Breath"
(*WOYC*, 17), establishes similar correspondences between

"place," "home," and "self" and describes, in a particularized context, the process of self-redefinition traced in "The Farm on the Great Plains." The entire process, as Stafford portrays it here, takes place in a single moment, while he hesitates before entering his parents' house. The poem reads:

> The night my father died the moon shone on the snow.
> I drove in from the west; mother was at the door,
> All the light in the room extended like a shadow.
> Truant from knowing, I stood where the great dark fell.
>
> There was a time before, something we used to tell—
> how we parked the car in a storm and walked into a field
> to know how it was to be cut off, out in the dark alone.
> My father and I stood together while the storm went by.
>
> A windmill was there in the field giving its little cry
> while we stood calm in ourselves, knowing we could go home.
> But I stood on the skull of the world the night he died, and knew
> that I leased a place to live with my white breath.
>
> Truant no more, I stepped forward and learned his death.

The first stanza establishes, with symbolic overtones such as "moon" and "snow," the poem's setting and occasion. "Truant" is intended both in its modern sense and in its archaic sense of "wretched." "Truant from knowing" is thus a terse phrase to express one's initial reaction to a death: although the implications of the event and its finality cannot be immediately absorbed—one avoids "knowing"—he is wretched.

The second and third stanzas describe a jolting movement from childhood truancy to adulthood. The adult realization toward which the poem moves is that it was impossible to "know how it was to be cut off, out in the dark alone" while "knowing we could go home," while envisioning "home" as a literal, physical location to which one *could* "go." Stafford's metaphor of "home" as the "self" is buried in the line "while we stood calm in ourselves, knowing we could go home," where Stafford recollects with a somber chagrin his childhood sense of home and self as *distinct* "places." Stafford's adult recognition of the correspondence of "home" to "self" to "place" as identity is clinched in the expression "a place to live" in the last line. Stafford's sense of space has collapsed in upon him. "A place to live," one's "home," *is* the self, one's singular identity, and this is but "leased." Stafford's premonition of his own mortality is as keen in this line as in "My self will be the plain."

Another example of the equivalence which Stafford makes between "place," "self," and "home" may be seen in the opening of "Allegiances" (*A*, 77):

> It is time for all the heroes to go home
> if they have any, time for all us common ones
> to locate ourselves by the real things
> we live by.

In this passage, the contrast between "heroes" and "us common ones" is identical to the contrast which Stafford makes in "Deerslayer's Campfire Talk" between "the ones who . . . call the plans" and "ordinary men." "If they have any" is meant wryly but seriously; for "the ones . . . who call the plans" are "thinkers" who are "deaf to process." Since an individual's home can only be realized through process, the "heroes" may not have "selves."

The metaphor of "place" is implicit in the word "locate"; the concept of "self" is buried in "ourselves" which echoes "home" in the first line. Stafford's notion that "place" is defined through process is implicit in the fact that "locate" is a verb. The concept of "place" recurs in the conclusion of this poem: "we ordinary beings can cling to the earth and love/ where we are, sturdy for common things." "Love/ where we are" means simply "accept who we are."

Stafford's poem "Recoil" (*RY*, 80) relates "home" to process:

> The bow remembers home long,
> the years of its tree, the whine

of wind all night conditioning
it, and its answer—Twang!

To the people here who would fret me down
their way and make me bend:
*By remembering hard I could startle for home
and be myself again.*

Explicit here is Stafford's imagined assumption that the process
by which the self develops its temper is like the process by
which the wood of a tree develops its grain, that individual
human process has a natural analogue.

Since the self, like any identity, is defined through process,
Stafford's path metaphor forms an important component of
his vision of himself as an individual. "Reporting Back" (*TTD*,
31) defines "home" as a "place" on a "path," as that sense of
identity which one suffers at any given point in a continuous
but finite process:

By the secret that holds the forest up,
no one will escape. (We have reached this place.)

The sky will come home some day.
(We pay all mistakes our bodies make when they move.)

Is there a way to walk that living has obscured?
(Our feet are trying to remember some path we are walking toward.)

The "secret that holds the forest up" is the world's legend.
Although Nature ("the forest") supplies the clearest evidence
of this legend, the legend also comprehends the human domain:
"no one will escape." The "secret" *is* process: "We have
reached this place," this momentary identity defined by all
that we have done. "The sky will come home some day" is a
simple reminder that each of us will die: the self ("home")
and Nature ("the sky") will become identical. "We pay all
mistakes our bodies make when they move" is an ironical
rephrasing of "The world goes wrong in order to have revenge."

Although natural process as reflected in the human domain may be self-correcting, it is also mortal.

The last two lines introduce the metaphor of a path. As in "Walking the Wilderness," "living" is compared to "walking." The human individual, while he lives, is a "walker." "A way to walk" implies a prescribed process, one dictated by "the secret that holds the forest up." Like the dog in "An Epiphany," the walker cannot discern the path he is following. He keeps finding it as he goes along.

The poem's most ambiguous word is its last one: "toward." The sense in which Stafford intends it is "toward" completion. This usage is supported by the etymological link between "toward" and the Anglo-Saxon *weorþan*: "toward" means "to become." Our "feet," through the step-by-step process of "walking," are following a fixed but inexorable ("obscured") "path" toward completion. "The sky will come home some day" is a reminder that this path is finite. It will be completed when the walker dies. But so long as the walker is alive, is walking, his self will be defined only in proportion to that part of his prescribed path which he has already traveled or "remembered." Stafford's concept of the self, then, presents a paradox. Although the self is "fixed" with respect to its ultimate definition, until the walker stops walking, his self will be metamorphic.

The first stanza of "Late Thinker" contains a particularly beautiful image of the self "questioning one grain at a time,/ wandering like a dune." The self's configuration is, like the shape of a dune, continuously developing, one grain, one step at a time. The dune, like the self, is "wandering," changing "places": its identity is metamorphic.

Stafford's poem "Sophocles Says" (*RY, 76*), a poem which we can now read in its entirety, is about completion of the self:

> History is a story God is telling,
> by means of hidden meanings written closely
> inside the skins of things. Far over the sun
> lonesome curves are meeting, and in the clouds
> birds bend the wind. Hunting a rendezvous,

soft as snowflakes ride through a storm their pattern down,
men hesitate a step, touched by home.

A man passes among strangers; he never smiles;
the way a flame goes begging among the trees
he goes, and he suffers, himself, the kind of dark
that anything sent from God experiences,
until he finds through trees the lights of a town—
a street, the houses blinded in the rain—
and he hesitates a step, shocked—at home.

For God will take a man, no matter where,
and make some scene a part of what goes on:
there will be a flame; there will be a snowflake form;
and riding with the birds, wherever they are,
bending the wind, finding a rendezvous
beyond the sun or under the earth—that man
will hesitate a step—and meet his home.

"History" is the world's legend, the "dark . . . sent from God,"
as manifested in natural history, in collective human history
and in the history of the human individual. "Things"—all
elements of the world both human and natural—follow their
respective paths or "curves." "Lonesome" carries the sense of
singular or unique. "Curves" contains the connotation of
"bent": the curve which a "thing" follows is its natural bent.
When each "thing" dies, its path assumes its ultimate design: the "lonesome curve" it describes meets itself to form a
closed curve, a completed design like a "snowflake" with a
"pattern." "Snowflakes" here recalls "Walking the Wilderness":
"Snowflake designs lock; they . . ./ hold their patterns one by
one, down,/ spasms of loneliness." The snowflake is an emblem
of the completed path of the self. "Rendezvous," then, has a
double meaning. In its modern sense, "rendezvous" is synonymous with "meeting"—the meeting of a curve upon itself to
complete, upon the death of some "thing," the closed configuration of its identity. "Rendezvous," taken etymologically, suggests death-by-drowning, a *rendering* of the self back to the
earth.

The poem's second stanza suggests that the path of the individual walker is as fixed and inexorable as the world's legend. A man does not willfully choose it; he "suffers" it, or, as the end of the first stanza says, he is "touched by" it, impelled by "home," by a "dark . . . sent from God." The second stanza's last line, a variation upon the last line of the first stanza, establishes the same paradox developed in "Reporting Back": each "step" which a man "hesitates" *is* "home" in the sense that he has "reached this place," has realized his identity to the maximum extent possible at a given moment. The poem's last stanza, which is a redundant iteration of the material above it, relates the word "meet" in its last line to "meeting" in the fourth line of the first stanza. "Meet his home" synthesizes the end-lines of the preceding two stanzas into one paradox and links that paradox with death. "Meet his home" suggests both the meeting of a curve upon itself and that the walker will "meet his home" in the earth when he dies.

Stafford's vision that "a man . . . suffers, himself, the kind of dark/ that anything sent from God experiences" finds expression in a number of poems. The third stanza of "The Wanderer Awaiting Preferment" (*TTD*, 93) proposes natural process as a model of how God's darkness may be manifested in the human walker: ". . . As trees/ drink dark through roots for their peculiar grain/ while meager justice applauds up through the grass,/ I calm the private storm within myself." The "peculiar grain" of every element in the world is determined through a "dark" law.

In the second stanza of "Right Now" (*RY*, 64), Stafford describes how this "dark" is manifested in himself: "Led by my own dark I go/ my unmarked everlasting round/ frozen in this moment." The metaphor of process as path is implicit in the word "unmarked." The walker is led by God's "dark" along an unmarked path which, as the beginning of "Sophocles Says" indicates, is "written closely inside" him.

So long as the walker's path is *inside* him, it is "dark"; it must be imagined. The path becomes *visible* only as it is manifested through his actions, through outward gestures, through the process of "walking." The uncompleted segment of the walker's patterned path, invisible while inside him, writes itself out as a visible legend in the externalized marks he leaves behind him, the sum of his perfected gestures, dark process made visible. Since the "snowflake design" of his fully realized path or self will only be completed upon his death, while alive he will never apprehend a vision of his self's ultimate configuration. At any given "place" he has "reached" on his path, the only part of the path which will be visible to him will be that segment he has already traversed, the marks, the tracks he has left. As Stafford expresses this paradox in "With My Crowbar Key" (*TTD*, 17):

> I do tricks in order to know:
> careless I dance,
> then turn to see
> the mark to turn God left for me.

The path ahead of the walker is unmarked. It appears *behind* him ("I . . . turn to see/ the mark . . .") in the imprints his steps have made. These "marks" are memories. The function of memory is as crucial to Stafford's vision as it is to Wordsworth's. The marks which the walker leaves behind are his best and only clue to his ultimate identity.

"Mark," in the passage above, also suggests "poem." The marks one leaves—one's record of his uncompleted self—may be fixed through the medium of language, through "tricks." By ordering and containing memory, poetry can help define the shape of sloughed process. "The Farm on the Great Plains" and "Circle of Breath," for example, are emblems of the self seeking definition in the shape of past process. In "Report from a Far Place" (*SM*, 66), Stafford actually compares his poems ("word things") to snowshoes: "Making these word things to/ step on across the world, I/ could call them snowshoes."

My Self Will Be the Plain

The imprint each step leaves is a faint yet distinct record of the walker's life, a pattern upon the cold.

In Stafford's poems, the metaphor of the self as a walker whose every step leaves a mark is frequently extrapolated through images of past time and completed action as negative space, as the concave imprint which the walker's feet have made upon the world's surface. Such images are most prevalent in *The Rescued Year,* whose theme is, as its title implies, the use of memory. In "Uncle George," for example, the phrase "I plow and belong" imagines the walker leaving behind him a concave wake or furrow. In "Walking the Wilderness," Stafford refers to "the roads/ birds fly, the channels their lives make—." *The Rescued Year* contains two poems in which Stafford explicitly develops a time-space duality by which he represents past time as negative space and memory as "concave."

In "From Eastern Oregon" (*RY*, 65), he uses the image of a fossil to symbolize the path that he imagines his self will have completed upon his death. The poem describes exploring a cave by flashlight, but transforms the exploration into an imagined journey to the domain of the world's legend, a journey "inside the skins of things." The poem is in three stanzas. The first two, which establish the time-space duality, read as follows:

Your day self shimmers at the mouth of a desert cave;
then you leave the world's problem and find
your own kind of light at the pool that glows far back
where the eye says it is dark. On the cave wall
you make not a shadow but a brightness; and you can feel
with your hands the carved story now forgotten or ignored
    by the outside, obvious mountains.

Your eyes an owl, your skin a new part of the earth,
you let obsidian flakes in the dust discover your feet
while somewhere drops of water tell a rock.
You climb out again and, consumed by light, shimmer
full contemporary being, but so thin your bones

The Mark to Turn

register a skeleton along the rocks like
an intense, interior diamond.

Although the walker here is inside the earth, he is alive; his
journey is imagined. The walker and the world thus each
retain a distinct identity or "place." But since the walker is
inside the world, distance is an inoperable metaphor for the
distinction between them. The distinction is preserved instead
through images of light and darkness. The walker makes his
"own kind of light . . . where the eye says it is dark . . . not
a shadow but a brightness." "The carved story" which the
walker here can "feel," like the legend in "Bi-focal," has a
geological time-scale, one so immense that it is "dark"; it
dwarfs the time-scale of the mortal walker. The walker and
the world are thus differentiated with respect to their potential
for duration: what is "dark" has the potential for long duration; what "make[s] a brightness" is transitory. "Distance"—
distinction of identity—has thus been translated from spatial
into temporal terms. But the distance metaphor is still implicit.
The cave wall, as it reflects the "brightness" emanated by the
walker, becomes a bright surface which, by confronting him,
implies a physical distance between them. Time and space
are dual.

This duality is reversed when, in the second stanza, the
walker emerges. Whereas *inside* the earth he registered a
"brightness" on the cave wall, outside it the walker is confronted with a *bright* surface upon which his shadow is *dark*,
"but so thin" the "bones/ register a skeleton . . . like/ an intense, interior diamond." The primary distinction between the
walker and the world is now "spatial," but their distinction
with respect to time is preserved in the fossil image, which is
an emblem of rock's potential for longer duration. It will out-
last the walker, whose fossil is the image of his completed path
as a negative space, the concave snowflake design he will leave
upon the world.

Stafford's poem "Across the Lake's Eye" (*RY*, 69), one of
his most difficult poems, explicitly develops the metaphor of a

completed path as negative space. The poem, addressed to an imaginary "you" who is the spokesman for Stafford's imagination, reads as follows:

Walking ice across the lake's eye
to the deep and looking along the sight
at other worlds asleep for space
but not for light—
we came wide awake.
"Why close what eyes we have?" you said,

And "There's a left-hand world that other people see
that slinks aside from me,
that my dog hears;
the negative of the world, that suicides love;
that comes along the track from its pinpoint place;
that barely swerves beside our face
escaping either way outside our own,
beyond where night surprises the snow."

You made me look around that night.
And coming back you spun this left-hand story:
An island burrowed under the water
and rose pretending to be a different island
but a fish had followed it, making bubbles
wherever the island went. "Echoes,"
you said, "avoid that island now:
sound is dead there, but haunts the concave water
where the island used to be."

The world has character, you contended,
as we stamped home across the land,
making a record of that night,
marking the progress of an island.

The frozen lake is here an emblem of Nature at its coldest. With the help of his companion, Stafford is able to look at the "deep," at the way it is. The "other worlds" which he sees are the reflections of stars in the ice. "Asleep for space/ but not for light" refers to the fact that we may still see the light of stars which have already burnt out. "We came wide awake" is a rephrasing of "drowned awake" and "come to all at once in that/ dream" from "Walking the Wilderness." The light from dead stars in the ice at his feet is, for Stafford, an emblem of the fact that the dead who have passed into the ground still live in the memory. As Stafford phrases it in "Long Distance": "You think they are." The lake is a shiny graveyard. Stafford's imagination asks, "Why close what eyes we have?" It prompts him to philosophize:

In the second stanza, Stafford's companion speculates in a highly cryptic way about paths. The "left-hand world," "the negative of the world" (the "channel" which the walker leaves behind him) "comes along" a "track." The walker's path is one which "other people see" better than he can, because the wake he leaves opens up *behind* him and because, as "Reporting Back" suggests, the "track" "toward" which "we are walking" is one which "living has obscured." Although the path is prescribed, the walker cannot discern that segment of it which lies before him; each point along it "comes . . . from its pin-point place." As the last three lines suggest, the walker is making a path as though he were parting snow. The snow "swerves," "escaping" on either side of him. "Night surprises the snow" is a cryptic prefiguration of the poem's final image of the walker's "dark" "marking" the snow. "Beyond" means "behind."

In the third stanza, Stafford's companion shifts his ground and spins a parable which is directly related to the earlier star image. As "burrowed under water" suggests, the parable is about death, the death of any particular element of the world, human or natural. "Island" implies a circumscribed "place" and therefore any discrete identity. "An island burrowed under water/ and rose pretending to be a different island" means simply "something died and assumed another identity."

The remainder of the stanza alludes directly to "The Animal That Drank Up Sound." " 'Echoes [the imagination, the memory] . . . avoid that island now [that it has lost its original identity]:/ sound is dead there.' " Because the identity of a dead person is unimaginable, the imagination " 'haunts the concave water/ where the island used to be' ": one remembers the dead as they were when they were alive. Memories of the dead in the ground persist like the reflection of a dead star in the ice. These are, like the light which the star once made, memories of the completed path, the fossil which the dead person made while alive, "concave," visible imprints in the snow, markings upon the cold face of the world.

The poem's last stanza synthesizes the path images in the second stanza and the memory parable in the third. "Character," which is echoed by "stamped," is used in its Greek sense as "an engraved or stamped mark." It is also a pun. The visible, concave path which the walker's steps leave upon the world is the stamping of his character upon it. In the last line, both syllables of "island" are puns. An "island" is "my place." "Marking the progress of an island" is the legending of the process of my self.

5 The Mark to Turn

Stafford's poem "With My Crowbar Key" (*TTD*, 17) not only equates the act of writing with the process of self-definition; it suggests that through "tricks" one can glimpse, however momentarily, the dark process of the self "at work":[1]

> I do tricks in order to know:
> careless I dance,
> then turn to see
> the mark to turn God left for me.
>
> . . . .
>
> And by night like this I turn and come
> to this possible house
> which I open, and see
> myself at work with this crowbar key.

The word "tricks" recalls "Love the Butcher Bird Lurks Everywhere" (*TTD*, 62): "and willows do tricks to find an exact place in the wind." Both Stafford's "tricks" and the "tricks" which a willow does comprise the processes whereby they define their respective identities, their "place[s]." "This possible house" is a disguised reference to home, to "myself" in the last line. It is only a "possible" self, a temporary place on a path. Stafford's "tricks," however, differ from the willow's. They not only enable him to "come/ to this possible house"; they enable him to "open" it "and see/ myself at work." Human process is intrinsically self-conscious. Through writing, the human identity may continuously transcend itself. Human process, then, though analogous to natural process, may be distinguished from it by the fact that human process comprehends the potentiality not only to "find" a "place" but "to know."

In "The Gift" (*A*, 22), Stafford is more explicit. Writing is a way by which he "salvages" his "home":

> The writer's home he salvages from little pieces
> along the roads, from distinctions he remembers,
> from what by chance he sees—his grabbed heritage;
> and from people fading from his road, from history.

We recall that "home" is Stafford's primary metaphor for the self, and that Stafford envisions the self as a pattern which is gradually revealed and continuously defined through process, for which his primary metaphor is that of a path. In the lines above, the metaphor of path as process is implicit in "roads." The curious use of "heritage" in the third line contains the suggestion that the self's legend is prescribed: it is the writer's birthright, an *a priori* design which, "from distinctions he remembers," must be "grabbed" before it fades.

The organic relationship between the self and art suggested by Stafford's poems is a relationship of which he is wholly conscious and which forms the basis of his poetics. In his published lecture, "The Hues of English," for example, Stafford says: "For an artist, the materials of his activity become the partners of the self, and with a wonderfully free kind of reverberation the artist embarks on a process that eventuates in something new, unprecedented, 'original.' "[2]

In the *Prairie Schooner* interview, Stafford suggests an even more literal equivalence between his poems and his self: ". . . when I start to write, I would like to make myself available for every little nuance involved in an experience. In this way, the activity itself will be creative. Instead of feeling that I have to become a certain kind of person before I write, I'd like to accomplish the thing by the writing."[3]

It is evident from the passages above that Stafford envisions the "activity" of writing as being, for him, a wholly organic manifestation of the self. The self becomes what it legends. Paradoxically, however, it does not know in advance what it is going to become. It is through submission to "activity" that it "finds" its new "place" and is able to "see" itself "at work." It moves forward along its path, suffering a process of continuous transcendence. In his short essay, "Finding the Language," Stafford refers to writing both as "forward" movement and as "living the language": "And in writing I find that my practice initially is to roam forward through experience, finding the way as the process unfolds. This way with the language is interesting to me, and I believe such readiness is valid for living the language as we use it."[4] Writing, like walking, consists of "finding the way as the process unfolds," or, as Stafford expresses it in the *Field* essay, "following a process that leads . . . wildly and originally into new territory" toward what the self is becoming.[5]

Two of the metaphors which Stafford uses in his poems for this "new territory" are the words "west" and "wilderness." Both rely upon our historical and mythical sense of the west as a frontier, a wilderness which, because it is unexplored, can only be imagined. Both "west" and "wilderness" are used this way in Stafford's long poem "In Sublette's Barn" (*A*, 14-16), where, through the story of an imagined westward journey by a solitary mountain scout named "Sublette," Stafford presents an allegory of the self's continuous but sometimes fearful journey forward through process into fresh creation.[6]

A shorter and more explicit example of Stafford's use of the "west" motif is the title poem of *West of Your City* (*WYOC*, 10):

> *West of your city into the fern*
> *sympathy, sympathy rolls the train*
> *all through the night on a lateral line*
> *where the shape of game fish tapers down*
> *from a reach where cougar paws touch water.*

> . . . .

> *Cocked in that land tactile as leaves*
> *wild things wait crouched in those valleys*
> *west of your city outside your lives*
> *in the ultimate wind, the whole land's wave*
> *Come west and see; touch these leaves.*

Stafford wrote this poem in a train traveling east to Yaddo, the writers' colony in New York State. In context, however, the direction of the train is west, toward that "new territory" which will define the self. The reader is invited to "Come west" and, by "sympathy," to join the poet. The organic partnership which Stafford envisions between "art" and the self is implied in the last line: "these leaves" are the leaves of the book, the poems following the title poem. They are the marks which the self has left behind it in its westward journey. Implicit in the leaf metaphor is Stafford's appeal to his natural model as a rationale for poetry. The process through which the self has put forth "these leaves" is analogous to the process by which a tree manifests its foliage: it is integral to the self's existence.

A longer and more difficult poem, "Lake Chelan" (*TTD*, 50), makes a more explicit appeal. The first of the poem's five stanzas reads:

> They call it regional, this relevance—
> the deepest place we have: in this pool forms
> the model of our land, a lonely one,
> responsive to the wind. Everything we own
> has brought us here: from here we speak.

Although "Chelan" is the name of an actual lake located in the Cascades of northern Washington, in this poem Stafford uses the lake for wholly symbolic purposes. It is both an emblem of Nature and of the individual human self, "the deepest place we have." "Our land" is used here as "island" is used in "Across the Lake's Eye." "The deepest place" which we can imagine in the natural world is "the model of our" place, our self. "Everything we own/ has brought us here: from here we speak" establishes the poem's theme as the relationship between poetry, the self, and Nature. The word "regional" in the first line alludes to the fact that Stafford has frequently been labeled a "regional" poet.[7] The entire poem is an argument against this label which "They" have applied.

The second stanza imagines the lake "lost by a century" and on it a "ferryboat" which "toots/ for trappers." The poem's last three stanzas read as follows:

> Suppose a person far off to whom this lake
> occurs: told a problem, he might hear a word
> so dark he drowns an instant, and stands dumb
> for the centuries of his country and the suave
> hills beyond the stranger's sight.
>
> Is this man dumb, then, for whom Chelan lives
> in the wilderness? On the street you've seen
> someone like a trapper's child pause,
> and fill his eyes with some irrelevant flood—
> a tide stops him, delayed in his job.
>
> Permissive as a beach, he turns inland,
> harks like a fire, glances through the dark
> like an animal drinking, and arrives along that line
> a lake has found far back in the hills
> where what comes finds a brim gravity exactly requires.

Stafford is here arguing that, through their adherence to a natural model ("Lake Chelan"), his poems have more than "regional" relevance. He is able to "suppose" that "this lake" may "occur" to "a person far off," to an audience remote from him and, taking "far off" to signify "different," to a person different from himself.

The first sentence of the fourth stanza is an ironically phrased rhetorical question. "This man" may refer either to the poet or to the "person far off." If it refers to the poet, then "Is this man dumb . . . ?" asks whether it is foolish to take seriously "a word/ so dark" one "drowns an instant." If "this man" refers to "a person far off," then the question refers to the fact that, although the "person . . . to whom this lake/ occurs" may be "dumb"—unable to express the dark word—it is the job of the poet to speak for him.

The remainder of the fourth stanza hypothesizes a larger audience. "Someone like a trapper's child" could, in context, be anyone, since figuratively we are all descendants of the "trappers" of a century ago. "Irrelevant flood," which echoes "relevance" in the poem's first line, is ironical. What rises from "the deepest place we have" may be irrelevant to our "job," but it is wholly relevant to the self.

The last stanza attributes to the processes of the self a propriety as rigorous as the justice which Stafford imagines in the natural world. When a "trapper's child" "turns inland" to his deepest place, he submits to a natural justice as strict and pure as the forces which govern the water level of a lake. No matter how "regional," how apparently circumscribed one's deepest place is, it has an unlimited relevance because, as Stafford imagines, it partakes of a darkness sent by God, gravity, which transcends the particular. When "we speak" from our "deepest place," we speak to everybody, no matter how "far off."

As so many of Stafford's poems do, "Lake Chelan" also recommends a posture of passive acquiescence in process. If we take "regional" and "relevance" in their Latin senses, then the poem may be construed as a rebuttal to the possibility of a deliberately written, intellectually conceived poetry, to poetry written with a definite, prescribed end in mind. "They call it regional, this relevance" carries the distinct suggestion, "They call it governable, this rising up [of a poem]." As we recall, poetry for Stafford is "the stance that accepts," a stance which in "Lake Chelan" is "responsive to the wind," "Permissive as a beach." If one submits to process, then when he writes, "what comes" must find "a brim gravity exactly requires." "Lake Chelan," however, poses a paradox which is hard to ignore and one which Stafford's poems present repeatedly. Although "Lake Chelan" argues that poetic composition is an essentially organic, intuitive process, the poem exhibits a good deal of conscious artifice: a scrupulous regard for New Critical "tension";[8] the use of "deep" and "dark" as counters in a symbolic shorthand which is logically consistent; the etymological use of words like "relevance" to admit a carefully *limited* ambiguity. Some of its lines are in iambic pentameter, and the poem is broken into five five-line stanzas, each of which represents a discrete block in an argument. Although this argument is figurative and compressed, its development is logical, each stanza-break serving as an orderly transition. In no way does "Lake Chelan" look spontaneous. It is rhetorically contrived. It is, as Stafford puts it in an interview with *Trace*, "considered" speech.[9] Indeed, although many of Stafford's poems look backward to Wordsworth, to Thoreau, to the organicism endemic to so much of the Romantic tradition, their form seems to contradict this sentiment. This apparent contradiction is sharpened by Stafford's own statements about his craft. Invariably he portrays himself as more of an organicist than he really is. In the *Prairie Schooner* interview, for example, Stafford says, "I feel reluctant somehow to learn a technique of poetry without having to. There is a different kind of progression that I would rather follow; maybe it is an organic development."[10]

With Stafford, "organic development" takes the appropriate form of a "journal." In the *Trace* interview, where Stafford mentions this "journal," he insists rather shrilly that his poetry is not willed, that it simply manifests itself as regularly and naturally as a tree manifests leaves: "I write prose and poetry all the time in what I guess could be called my journal—some writing almost every day. From the journal, I take certain interesting things and make poems of them—or just take them out, *already poems*. I don't aim a poem—consciously."[11] Consistent with his claim that his poems are not consciously "aimed" is Stafford's assertion that for him the process of composition is an end in itself. In the *Courier* interview, for example, where he discusses the limitation of "political" poems, Stafford says:

> There are problems for all of us, I think, in writing under conditions that force us or induce us to be purposeful about ends outside of the process itself. The process itself is imaginative; if you have a program before you start to write, it's not imaginative. I mean just that far you've inhibited the process. So it's dangerous, inhibiting, or stultifying to be under too great a pressure for delivering a message, it seems to me.[12]

Stafford's stance with respect to organicism is similar to Emerson's. Unwilling to undertake the radical experiments of a Thoreau, unable to let form relax into the plasticity which we associate with truly "organic" forms such as *Leaves of Grass*, Stafford remains like Emerson a professional man of letters who lays claim to the American transcendental tradition by sympathy. Both are cheering spectators, yet both want a more active role. It is no accident that both Stafford and Emerson (like Wordsworth) use essentially the same argument to claim this role: after identifying "poetry" with the organic, they try to break down the distinction between "poetry" and "prose." For example, in the *Prairie Schooner* interview, Stafford says: "My stance as a writer . . . is that writing is very much like talking. It's easy. We're all adept at talking. But many of us have been stampeded into believing there's some huge threshold to be surmounted before we can cross into writing. What I want to plead for is a reduction of apprehension about that threshold. . . ."[13] This argument, which culminates in a notion similar to Emerson's notion of language as "fossil poetry," posits an organic connection between language and human activity; language is, figuratively, one of the elements in which we live and move: "All of us know how to swim in the language; . . . But meanwhile there exist always those sleeping resources in language—connotations, sound reinforcements, allusions, myth-residues, and so on. These elements flicker on and off in anything we say or write, be it prose or poetry. Poets try to live up to these resources."[14] The poet, Stafford argues, is merely an adept, experienced swimmer: "When you make a poem you merely speak or write the language of every day, capturing as many bonuses as possible and economizing on losses: that is, you come awake to what always goes on in the language. . . ."[15] As a specific example of the "bonuses" of the "sleeping resources" in language, Stafford offers the following: "Consider a group of words like slide, slither, slick, sludge . . . We could all slosh our way to some slimy convergence of feeling in that group. Or consider skid, ski, skate, scat. . . ."[16] Stafford is arguing that *any* latent concreteness in language is "poetry." The obvious conclusion to this argument may be found in Stafford's short essay, "Some Arguments Against Good Diction," where he says: "Even if what we write is prose, we may speak of it or identify it with 'the poetical.' I take 'poetical' to mean in this context that there is some kind of dynamism in the language itself. . . ."[17] For Stafford, then, poetry is but one strand of a larger process of involvement in language. Like Wordsworth, Stafford sees no "*essential* difference between the language of prose and metrical composition."

If we accept this leveling of poetry and prose, then our objection that the disciplined form of Stafford's poems denies their content becomes trivial; for if poetry is merely one aspect of talking, and if talking is as endemic to human nature as swimming is to a fish, who can object if Stafford views the activity of writing as an organic process.

But Stafford's comparison between "writing" and "swimming" suggests not only the similarities between man and fish: it suggests the differences. Indeed, as we have seen, it is Stafford's steady awareness of a felt *difference* between himself and

Nature which radically distinguishes his Romanticism from that of his predecessors. In Stafford's poems, although Nature evinces both a consciousness and a strict propriety of process, Nature doesn't afford Stafford any of the "tranquil restoration" that it affords Wordsworth; it is merely "the cold with eyes." And the landscape of justice contains few prescriptions definite enough to be useful guides to human behavior. It provides only distant analogues. So long as we are alive, Nature is "far" from where we are. When we die, we become it again. Stafford's poems grimly acknowledge this, but they do not, like Whitman's, celebrate the final identification. If they celebrate anything, they celebrate the difference between man and Nature, a difference that is grounded in our language; for it is language itself that distinguishes the human walker from the world, allows the human individual to walk upon it, to *know*. The activity of talking or writing, then, is "organic" only insofar as it is endemic to the *human* organism.

The first two stanzas of "Report From a Far Place" (*SM*, 66) epitomize Stafford's view of both the function of language and the function of poetry in defining the human "place":

> Making these word things to
> step on across the world, I
> could call them snowshoes.
>
> They creak, sag, bend, but
> hold, over the great deep cold,
> and they turn up at the toes.

Like the snowshoes, language (particularly poetry) protects the walker from "ultimate identification," from sinking into "the great deep cold." The elements of conscious craft, of logical development, of prosodic regularity in Stafford's poems are reflected in the beautiful image of the snowshoe—a grid or array of thongs which is essentially regular yet which is fabricated from natural materials, from wood and leather. The "snowshoes" "creak, sag, bend"; they're flexible enough to cover various kinds of terrain, are reasonable without being rigidly

The Mark to Turn

76

formalistic, solid without being sterilely neoclassical. "Report From a Far Place" describes exactly that balance of meter and free verse, of precision yet indirection, of symbolic richness but logical clarity that distinguishes "Lake Chelan." If "these word things" were not so flexible, they would break. They would not work.

"Report From a Far Place" is a relatively abstract poem, relying heavily upon Stafford's symbolic shorthand. A less theoretical poem is "How I Escaped" (*A*, 60). Here, as in "Report From a Far Place," walking is a metaphor for the activity of writing. Stafford's metaphor for the human order inherent in language and in poetry is that of a "cage."

> A sign said "How to Be Wild—
> the Lessons Are Free,"
> so I edged past, bolted inside
> carefully,
> where the edge of a jaguar
> roved beyond bars
> and narrowed the room. Its head,
> one eye at a time,
> sewed the tent to the stars; and the cage
> ballooned when he turned.
>
> Mid-stride, I froze and stared
> past enemies
> that fell in droves down aisles
> of my memories.
> My bones—wild flowers—burned
> at whatever I'd lost,
> but my enemies burned up too
> in that holocaust;
> and I strode on, caged from them
> in disregard,
> swerving, momently aimed,
> like a jaguar.
>
> Though calm now, made to forgive
> by bars between,

> still fitted in those paw gloves
> I walk what I mean.

In the first stanza, the poet tries to learn through the imagination "How to Be Wild," he tries to reconstruct the consciousness of a jaguar. The last three lines of this stanza suggest that the jaguar does not finely differentiate what it perceives and that each moment of its conscious life is absolute and eternal: it lives "one eye at a time," and everything which it perceives is, like the "tent" and the "stars," "sewed" together.

In the second stanza, Stafford speaks both for himself and for the jaguar. "My bones—wild flowers—burned/ at whatever I'd lost" means: 1. that the jaguar which is in captivity has lost something because it is not in its natural habitat, it is no longer "wild"; 2. the poet feels that, compared to the jaguar, he—a civilized human being—may also have "lost" something. The last four lines establish a momentary ambiguity. If "I" refers to the jaguar, "them" means the human beings outside the cage. If "I" refers to the poet, "them" refers to his enemies: Stafford cannot hurt *his* "enemies" because he is "caged from them" by language; through the jaguar, he can terrify them in his imagination until his attitude is merely "disregard." "I strode on" thus carries a strong suggestion of transcendence, of moving *beyond* the limitations of "that holocaust."

The last stanza completes Stafford's metaphor of language as cage. The difference between human beings and jaguars is that human beings are "made to forgive." This difference is epitomized by the "bars" which separate the jaguar from us. The bars symbolize the containing and transcendent power of language, of poetry. They define a distinction between the natural world and the human domain. By imaginatively climbing into the cage, Stafford is able both to achieve "calm" and to remain human. Having caged his "holocaust," he can stand back and observe his own poem as he would stand back and look at a caged jaguar.

Stafford's cage "balloons," but, like his snowshoes, it will hold. Inside it are the steps of the walker like the fresh prints of an animal, marks to turn sent the walker from God. So long as there are "bars" between the human and the holocaust; so long as the creaking thongs of language support the walker westward over the great deep cold, he can speak, he can "know," he is still human. He can say, as Stafford truly does: "I walk what I mean."

Notes

CHAPTER 1
INTRODUCTION

1. William Stafford, "A Way of Writing," *Field* 2 (1970): 11.
2. In an interview with Sam Bradley ("Reciprocity vs. Suicide," *Trace* 3 [1962]: 223), Stafford estimated that "at least seven-eighths" of his poems have not been published. In conversation with me, he estimated that his books contain perhaps a quarter of his published poems. Stafford, of course, keeps his own records of which poems have appeared where. The largest public record available is the steadily growing collection of everything published by or about Stafford which is being compiled and indexed by James Pirie of the Lewis and Clark College Library. Pirie's bibliography is the best available.
3. Although it was published by a small press in a limited edition of several hundred, *West of Your City* (Los Gatos, California: Talisman Press, 1960) attracted significant critical attention.
4. "An Informal Discussion with William Stafford," *Courier* 19, no. 2 (February 1971): 6.
5. Karen Sollid, "William Stafford: Sunflowers Through the Dark," *Organon* 2 (Fall 1970): 67–70.
6. Ibid., pp. 64–65.
7. *The New Poets* (New York: Oxford University Press, 1967), p. 319.
8. Lewis Turco and Gregory Fitz Gerald, "Keeping the Lines Wet: A

Conversation with William Stafford," *Prairie Schooner* 44 (Summer 1970): 123–126.

9. "Tact" is a term I recall from Snodgrass's lecture "Tact and the Poet's Force" which I attended over a decade ago.

CHAPTER 2
BI-FOCAL

1. *Prairie Schooner* 44: 129–130.
2. *Courier* 19, no. 2: 7.
3. For example, in "Traveling through the Dark" (*TTD*, 11), line 16 reads: "around our group I could hear the wilderness listen."

CHAPTER 3
THE EARTH SAYS—

1. William Stafford, "At Home On Earth," *Hudson Review* 23 (Autumn 1970): 481.
2. "Reduplication of mirage" may also refer to the writing of poetry. In the *Prairie Schooner* interview (44: 32), Stafford, describing the genesis of his poem "Traveling through the Dark," uses the expression "redoubling of experience": "The poem concerns my finding a dead deer on the highway. This grew out of an actual experience. . . . As I was recounting the story to my kids the next day, I discovered by the expressions on their faces that I was arriving at some area of enhancement in the narrative. It wasn't until I saw their expressions that I felt my narrative itself helping to produce a kind of redoubling of experience."
3. Stafford was a conscientious objector in World War II. *Down In My Heart*, his creative thesis for the master's degree at the University of Kansas, published in 1948 (rpt., 1971) by the Brethren Publishing House describes his experience in a Civilian Public Service work camp from 1940 to 1944.
4. In "Parentage" (*TTD*, 20), for example, Stafford says: "I want to be as dumb as the wise are wrong." Stafford's mockery of "wisdom" is even more pointed in "The Little Ways That Encourage Good Fortune" (*SM*, 56), which opens: "Wisdom is having things right in your life/ and knowing why." "Knowing why" things are right in your life is, of course, impossible. Stafford means that so-called "wisdom" is having things right in your life and believing (wrongly) that you know "why." The passage is satirical. Wisdom is a form of pride.

CHAPTER 5

THE MARK TO TURN

1. In the *Field* essay (2: 11), Stafford inadvertently explicates line two, "careless I dance," when he remarks: "I must be willing to fail. If I am to keep on writing, I cannot bother to insist on high standards. I must get into action . . . I am thinking about what many people would consider 'important' standards, . . . social significance, positive values, consistency, etc. I resolutely disregard these. . . . So, receptive, careless of failure, I spin out things on the page. . . ."

2. William Stafford, "The Hues of English," *NCTE Distinguished Lectures*, 1969, Champaign, Illinois, p. 4.

3. *Prairie Schooner* 44: 133.

4. William Stafford, "Finding the Language," in *Naked Poetry*, ed. Stephen Berg and Robert Mezey (New York: Bobbs-Merrill, 1969), p. 83.

5. *Field* 2: 11.

6. Although "Sublette" was the surname of a famous mountain scout, Stafford's poem is wholly independent of any historicity that its title might suggest.

7. For example, M. L. Rosenthal (*The New Poets*, p. 319) refers to "the elusively impressionistic William Stafford, whose poetry is unobtrusively regional."

8. When Stafford was attending the Iowa Writers Workshop in the early 1950s, the New Criticism was near the peak of its popularity.

9. *Trace* 3: 224.

10. *Prairie Schooner* 44: 134–135.

11. *Trace* 3: 224.

12. *Courier* 19, no. 2: 9.

13. *Prairie Schooner* 44: 130.

14. "The Hues of English," *NCTE Distinguished Lectures*, pp. 6–7.

15. Ibid.

16. Ibid.

17. William Stafford, "Some Arguments Against Good Diction," *New York Quarterly* 5 (Winter 1971): 111.

˜Bibliography˜

"An Informal Conversation with William Stafford." *Courier* 19, no. 2 (February 1971): 5–11.

"An Interview with William Stafford." *Crazy Horse* 7 (June 1971): 36–41.

"An Interview with William Stafford." *Iowa Review* 3, no. 3 (Summer 1972): 92–107.

Bradley, Sam. "Reciprocity vs. Suicide: Interview with William Stafford." *Trace* 3 (1962): 223–226.

Childress, William. "William Stafford" (an interview). *Poetry Now* 2, no. 2: 1–2, 37.

Coles, Robert. "William Stafford's Long Walk." *American Poetry Review* 4, no. 4 (1975): 27–28.

Greiner, Charles F. "Stafford's 'Traveling through the Dark.'" *English Journal* 60: 1015–1018.

Heyen, William. "William Stafford's Allegiances." *Modern Poetry Studies* 1 (1970): 307–318.

Howard, Richard. *Alone with America: Essays on the Art of Poetry in the United States*. New York: Atheneum, 1969.

Hugo, Richard. "Problems with Landscapes in Early Stafford Poems." *Kansas Quarterly* 2, no. 2: 33–38.

Kyle, Carol A. "Point of View in 'Returned to Say' and the Wilderness of William Stafford." *Western American Literature* 7: 191–201.

McMillan, Samuel H. "On Willliam Stafford and His Poems: A Selected Bibliography." *Tennessee Poetry Journal* 11 (Spring 1969): 21–22.

Moran, Ron. "The Emotive Imagination." *Southern Review* 3: 51–67.

"Keeping the Lines Wet: A Conversation with William Stafford." *Prairie Schooner* 44 (Summer 1970): 123–136.

Kelley, Patrick. "Legend and Ritual." *Kansas Quarterly* 2, no. 2: 28–31.

Pinsker, Sanford. "Finding What The World Is Trying To Be: A Conversation With William Stafford." *American Poetry Review* 4, no. 4 (1975): 28–30.

Roberts, J. Russell, Sr. "Listening to the Wilderness with William Stafford." *Western American Literature* 3, no. 3 (Fall 1968): 217–226.

Rosenthal, M. L. *The New Poets.* New York: Oxford University Press, 1967.

Stafford, William. "A Message to Writers and Everyone." *Etchings* 1 (Spring 1962): 15.

————. "A Way of Writing." *Field* 2 (Spring 1970): 10–14.

————. *Allegiances.* New York: Harper & Row, 1970.

————. "At Home on Earth." *Hudson Review* 23 (Autumn 1970): 481–491.

————. *Down in My Heart.* Elgin, Illinois: Brethren Publishing House, 1947 (rpt. 1971).

————. *Eleven Untitled Poems.* Mt. Horeb, Wisconsin: Perishable Press, 1969.

————. "Finding the Language." *Naked Poetry*, ed. Stephen Berg and Robert Mezey. New York: Bobbs-Merrill, 1969, pp. 82–83.

————. "Friends to This Ground; A Statement for Readers, Teachers and Writers of Literature." Champaign, Illinois: National Council of Teachers of English, 1967.

————. *Going Places.* Reno: The West Coast Poetry Review, 1975.

————. *In the Clock of Reason.* Soft Press: Victoria, B.C., 1973.

————. "Left Foot Hope, Right Foot Despair." Lewis and Clark College Commencement Address, June 2, 1963.

————. "Oberlin Commencement Address." *Oberlin Alumni* 67 (July/August 1971): 5–11.

————. "Some Arguments Against Good Diction." *New York Quarterly* 5 (Winter 1971): 109–112.

————. *Someday, Maybe.* New York: Harper & Row, 1973.

————. *Temporary Facts.* Athens, Ohio: Duane Schneider Press, 1970.

————. "Terror in Robert Frost." *New York Times Magazine*, August 18, 1974, pp. 24–26.

————. *The Achievement of Brother Antoninus.* Glenview, Illinois: Scott, Foresman, 1967.

—————. "The Farm on the Great Plains." *Poet's Choice,* ed. Paul Engle and Joseph Langland. New York: Dial Press, 1962, 143.

—————. "The Hues of English." *NCTE Distinguished Lectures, 1969* (Champaign, Illinois), pp. 2–9.

—————. *The Rescued Year.* New York: Harper & Row, 1966.

—————. *Traveling through the Dark.* New York: Harper & Row, 1962.

—————. *Weather.* Mt. Horeb, Wisconsin: Perishable Press, 1969.

—————. *West of Your City.* Los Gatos, California: Talisman Press, 1960.

————— and Robert Henry Ross, ed. *Poems and Perspectives.* Glenview, Illinois: Scott-Foresman, 1971.

Stepanchev, Stephen. *American Poetry Since 1945.* New York: Harper & Row, 1965.

Sumner, D. Nathan. "The Poetry of William Stafford: Nature, Time and Father." *Research Studies* 36: 187–195.

Index